Contents

General Directions

The Patterns

All of the blocks in this book are 7" finished. The full-color patterns have more than one section that must be foundation-pieced individually and then sewn together. Bold lines that are also the cutting lines indicate these sections, **Figure 1**. A piecing diagram is included with each block showing the piecing order of the sections.

Also included with each block pattern is a photograph showing the completed block. Note the finished blocks are mirror images of the original patterns.

Note: *To have your finished character face the opposite direction, reverse the design on your pattern before sewing.*

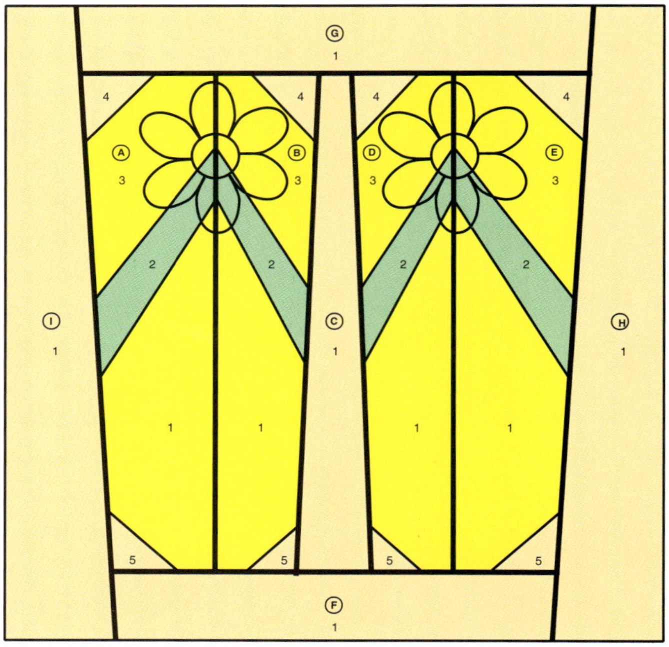

Fig. 1

Fabric

We recommend using 100 percent cotton fabric for piecing. By using cotton rather than cotton/polyester blends, the pieces will not slip as easily and will respond better to finger pressing.

Prewashing fabric is not necessary, but it is advisable to test your fabric to make certain that the fabric is colorfast (don't trust manufacturers' labels). Place a 2"-wide strip (cut crosswise) of fabric into a bowl of extremely hot water; if the water changes color, the fabric is bleeding and it will be necessary to wash that fabric until all of the excess dye has washed out. Repeat for all fabrics that will be used for your quilt. Fabrics that continue to bleed after they have been washed several times should be eliminated.

To test for shrinkage, take each saturated strip (used above in the colorfast test) and iron it dry with a hot iron. When the strip is completely dry, measure and compare it to your original 2" measurements. If all of your strips shrink about the same amount, then you really have no problem. When you wash your quilt, you may achieve the puckered look of an antique quilt. If you do not want this look, you will have to wash and dry all fabric before beginning so that shrinkage is no longer an issue. If any of your test strips are shrinking more than the others, these fabrics will need to be prewashed and dried, or discarded.

Embellishments

Some of the blocks have been enhanced with embellishments such as buttons, beads, acrylic jewels, ribbons, tassels, flowers and marker-drawn features.

Safety Note: *To eliminate the chance of a child's choking, do NOT use buttons, beads or small glued items on any quilt that will be handled by small children!*

In addition to items listed with the projects, you will find the following supplies helpful for embellishing your swatches:

- Glue
- Permanent fabric-marking pens
- Coordinating sewing thread

The Foundation-Piecing Method

Foundation Material

Before you start sewing, you need to decide the type of foundation on which to piece your blocks. There are several options. Paper is a popular choice for machine piecing because it is readily available and inexpensive. Copier paper works well, but newsprint found in office supply stores is much easier to handle since it is not as stiff. The paper is removed after the blocks are completely sewn.

Another alternative for foundation piecing is muslin or cotton fabric that is light colored and lightweight for easy tracing. The fabric will add another layer that you will have to quilt through, but that is only a consideration if you are going to hand-quilt. Also, if you use a fabric foundation, you will be able to hand-piece your blocks, if that is your desire.

A third option for foundation material is Tear Away® or Fun-dation™ translucent nonwoven material. Like muslin, it is light enough to see through for tracing, but like paper, it can be easily removed before quilting.

A new type of "disappearing" foundation material by W.H. Collins is called WashAway™ foundation paper. After sewing, place the block in water; the foundation dissolves in 10 seconds.

Preparing the Foundation

Tracing the Block

Trace the block pattern carefully onto your chosen foundation material. Use a ruler and a fine-point permanent marker or fine-line mechanical pencil to make straight lines; be sure to include all numbers and letters for multiple sections. Repeat for the number of blocks needed for your quilt.

Cutting the Fabric

One of the biggest advantages to foundation piecing is that you do not have to cut exact pieces for every block. This is especially important for smaller blocks or blocks with many small pieces. It is much easier to handle a small section or strip of fabric than it is to handle a triangle where the finished size of the sides is ¼".

The main consideration for using fabric pieces for a particular space is that the fabric must be at least ¼" larger on all sides than the space it is to cover. Squares and strips are easy to figure, but triangle shapes can be a little tricky to piece. Use generous-sized fabric pieces and be careful when positioning the pieces onto the foundation. You do waste some fabric this way, but the time it saves in cutting will be worth it in the end.

***Hint:** Measure the width of a particular space on your pattern; add ½" and cut a strip to that width, **Figure 2**. You will save time since you won't have to trim each seam allowance as you go.*

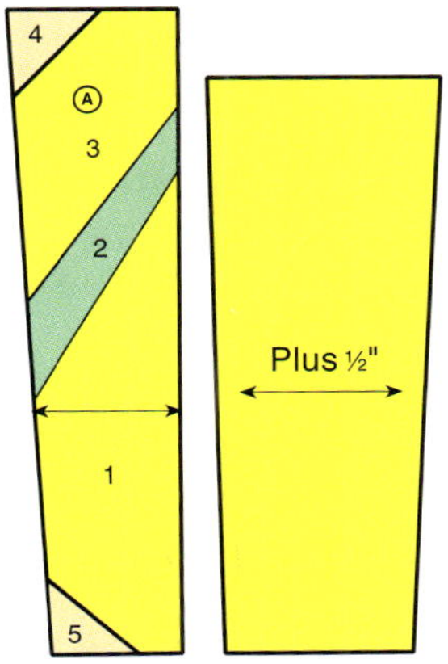

Fig. 2

How to Make a Foundation-Pieced Block

1. Prepare foundations as described on the previous page in Preparing the Foundation. Cut foundations apart along the bold lines to separate pattern into the smaller sections, **Figure 3**.

2. Starting with section A, turn the foundation section with the unmarked side facing you, and position piece 1 right side up over the space marked "1" on the foundation. Hold foundation up to a light source to make sure that fabric overlaps at least ¼" on all sides of space 1, **Figure 4**. Pin or use a glue stick to hold fabric in place.

***Hint:** Use only a small amount of a fresh glue stick to hold fabric in place. It is especially helpful to use a glue stick to keep larger or narrow pieces in place on the foundation until the blocks are sewn together.*

3. Turn foundation over. With marked side of foundation facing you, fold foundation forward along line between spaces 1 and 2, and trim fabric about ¼" from fold if needed, **Figure 5**.

4. Place fabric piece 2 right sides together with piece 1; edge of fabric 2 should be even with just-trimmed edge of fabric 1, **Figure 6**. Double-check to see if the fabric piece chosen will cover spaces 2 completely by folding over along line between space 1 and 2, **Figure 7**.

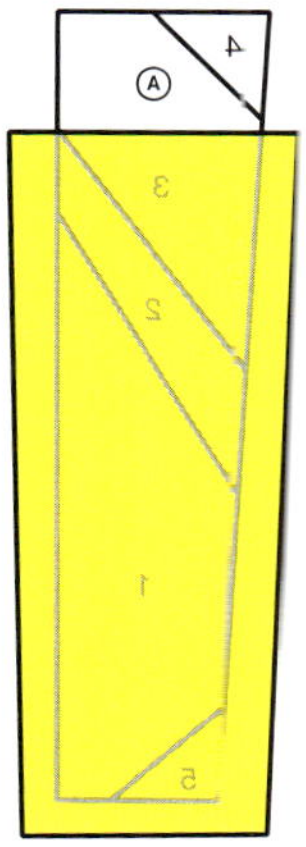

Fig. 4

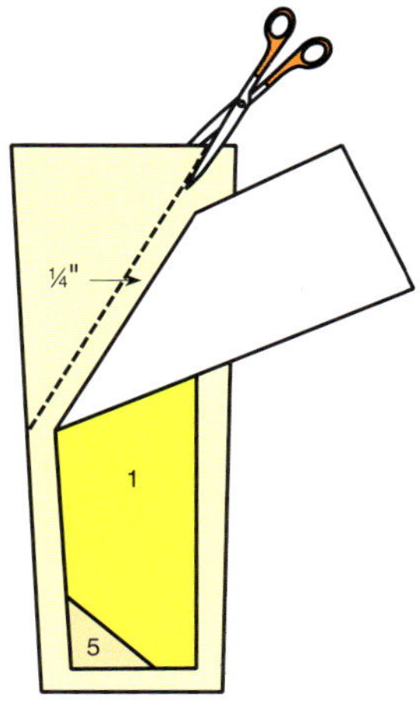

Fig. 5

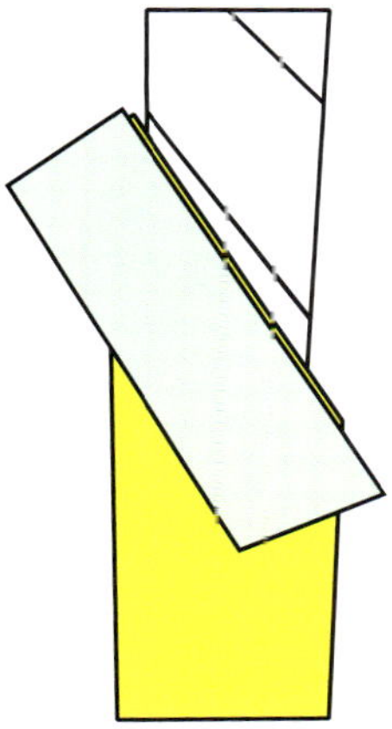

Fig. 6

Fig. 7

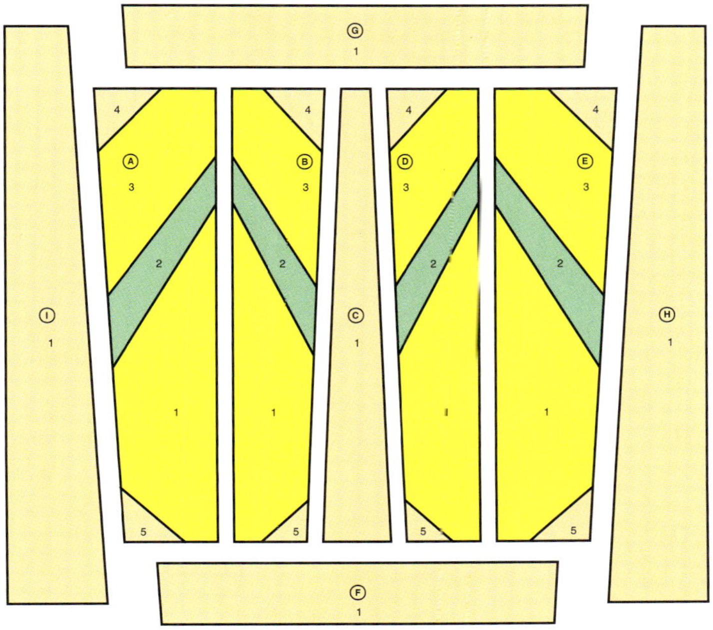

Fig. 3

5. With marked side of foundation facing you, place on sewing machine, holding fabric pieces together. Sew along line between spaces 1 and 2 using a very small stitch (18–20 stitches per inch), **Figure 8**. Begin and end sewing two to three stitches beyond line. You do not need to backstitch.

Hint: *Sewing with a very tiny stitch will allow for easier paper removal later. If paper falls apart after stitching, your stitch length is too small and you will need to lengthen the stitch slightly.*

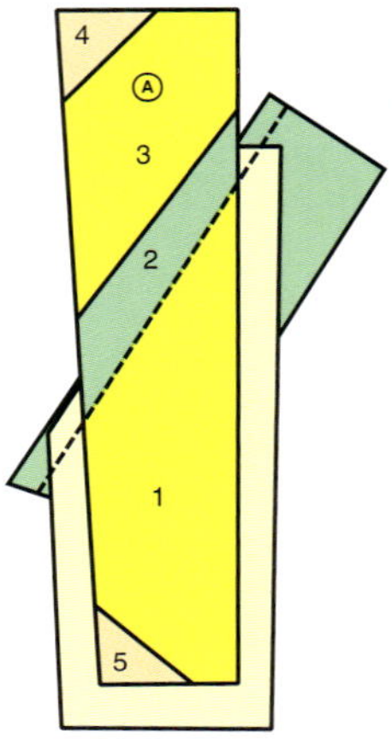

Fig. 8

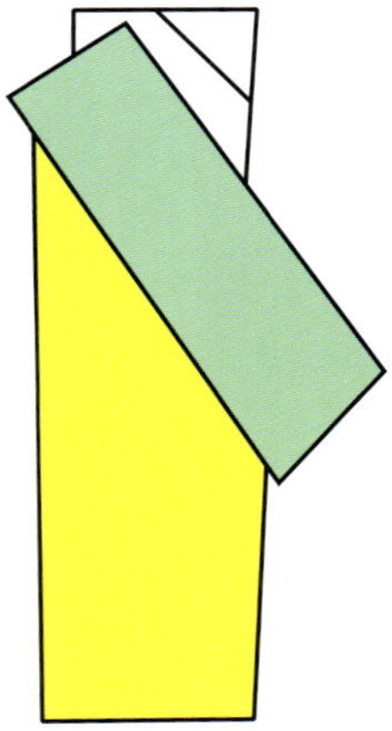
Fig. 9

6. Turn foundation over. Open piece 2 and finger-press seam, **Figure 9**. Use a pin or dab of glue stick to hold piece in place if necessary.

Hint: *If using strips, trim extra length being sure to leave enough to cover entire area plus seam allowance.*

7. Turn foundation with marked side of foundation facing you; fold foundation forward along line between spaces 2 and 3 and trim ¼" from fold if necessary, **Figure 10**.

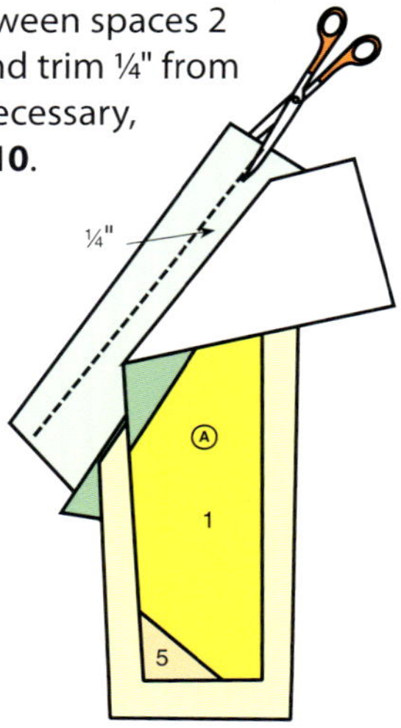

Fig. 10

8. Place fabric piece 3 right side down, even with just-trimmed edge, **Figure 11**.

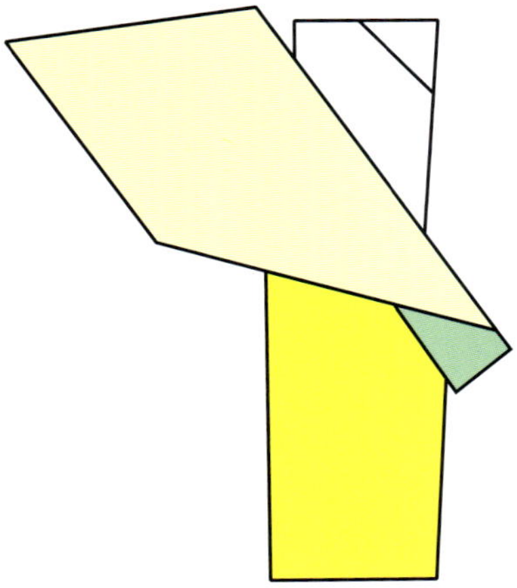
Fig. 11

9. Turn foundation to marked side and sew along line between spaces 2 and 3; begin and end sewing two to three stitches beyond line, **Figure 12**.

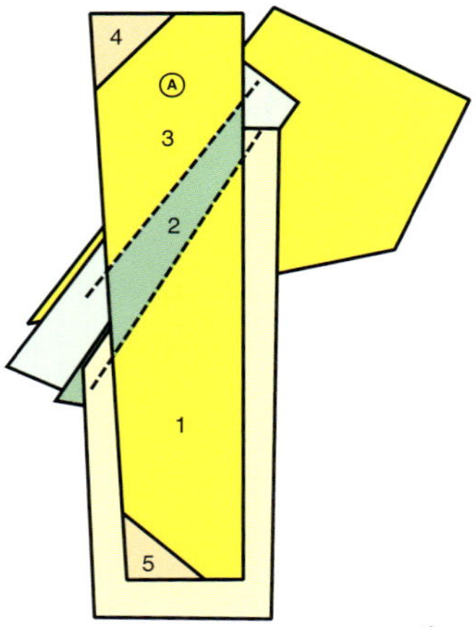

Fig. 12

10. Turn foundation over, open piece 3 and finger-press seam. Glue or pin in place, **Figure 13**.

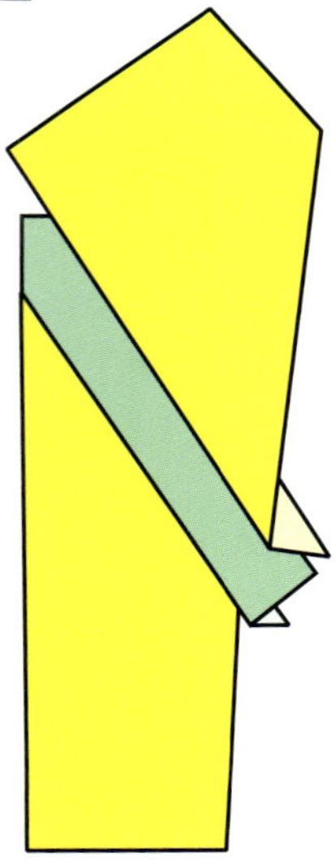
Fig. 13

11. Turn foundation with marked side facing you. Fold foundation forward along line between spaces 3 and 4; trim to about ¼" from fold, **Figure 14**.

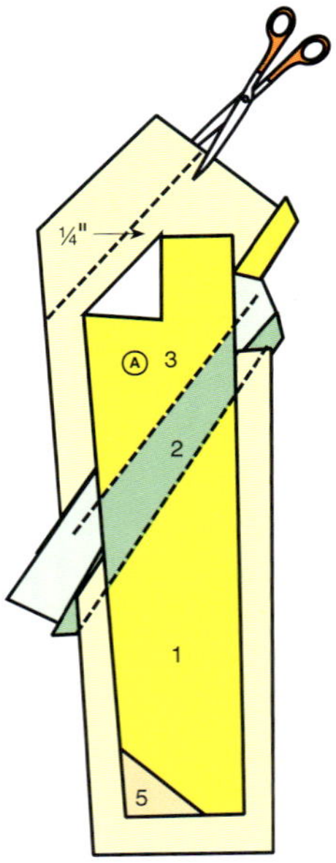

Fig. 14

Hint: *If using a paper foundation, carefully pull paper away from stitching for easier trimming. If using a fabric foundation, fold it forward as far as it will go and trim.*

12. Continue trimming and sewing pieces in numerical order until section is complete, **Figure 15**. Make sure pieces along the outer edge are large enough to allow for the ¼" seam allowance.

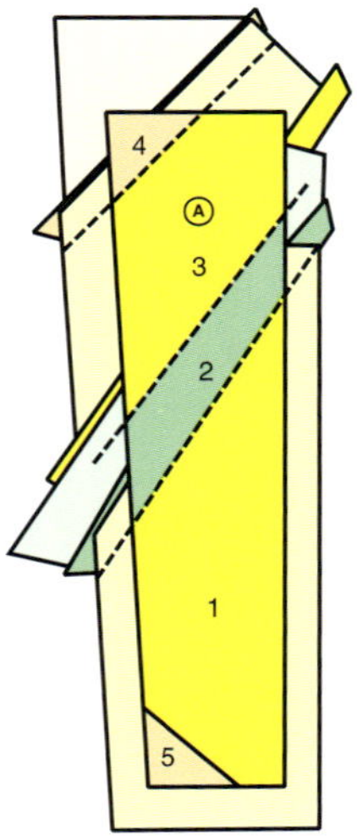

Fig. 15

13. Press, and then trim fabric ¼" from outside line of foundation to complete section, **Figure 16**.

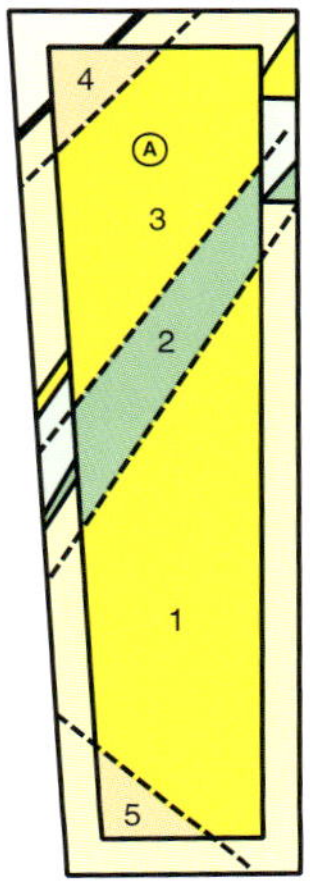

Fig. 16

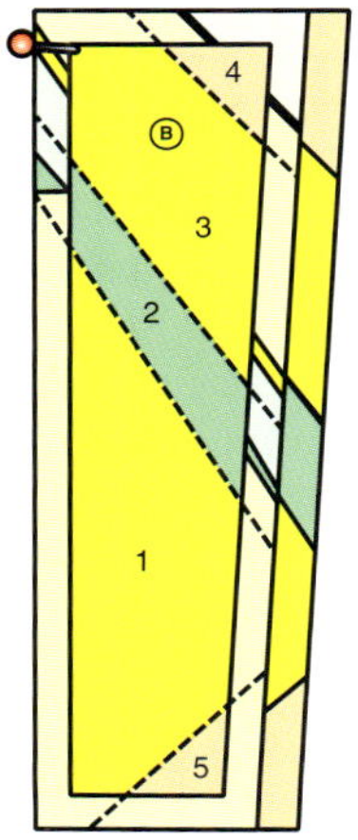

Fig. 17

14. Complete remaining sections of block in same manner.

15. Study the piecing diagram found on the pattern page. Sew sections in alphabetical order.

Note: *For some patterns, you may have to piece smaller sections before sewing to a previous section. For example, Man in the Moon (page 22) has sections A–K. Sew section A to B to C, and then set aside. Sew section D to E to F, then DEF to G. Sew ABC to DEFG, then sew to H, then to I. Continue in this manner.*

To sew sections, place right sides together; push a pin through corner of top section going through to corner of bottom section. Check to be sure pin goes through both corners and is perpendicular (going straight up) to section, **Figure 17**. If not, pin again until corners match.

Repeat at opposite end of seam line to match corners, **Figure 18**. It is also a good idea to pin the intersections of seams that should line up between the two sections.

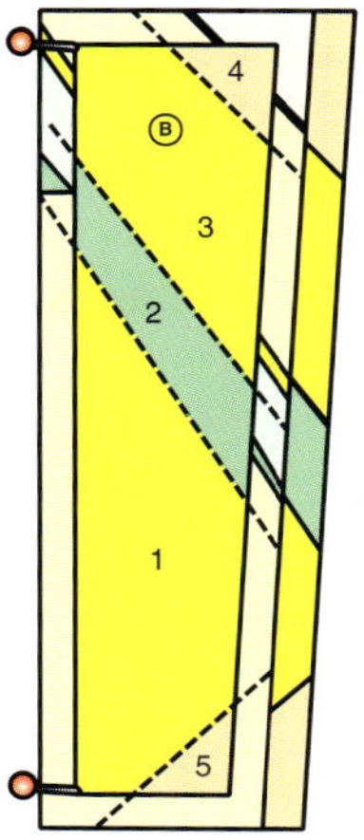

Fig. 18

Hint: *If desired, baste sections together by hand or machine. Check sections again; if everything matches up, sew together with regular stitches. Basting takes a little time, but the extra effort will be worth it in the end.*

16. Once pieces are lined up correctly, sew along edge of foundation using a regular stitch length, **Figure 19**.

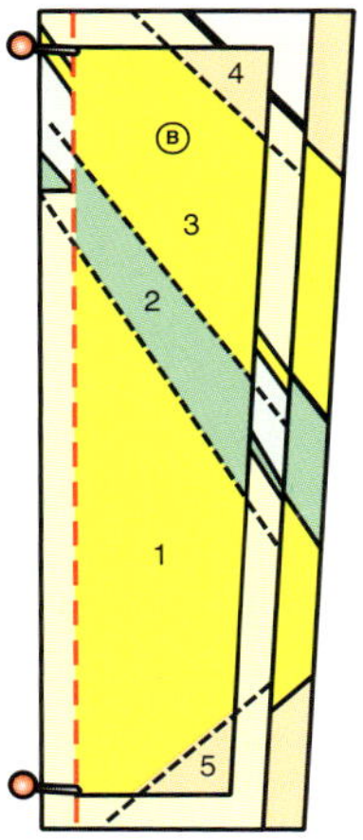

Fig. 19

17. Sew remaining sections together, referring to the order in the piecing diagram with each pattern.

Hint: *Do not remove paper yet. It is better to remove paper after blocks have been sewn together. Since grain line was not considered in piecing, outer edges may be on the bias and, therefore, stretchy. Keeping paper in place until after sewing will prevent the blocks from becoming distorted. Staystitching along outer edge of block,* ***Figure 20****, will also help keep fabric from stretching out of shape.*

Fig. 20

Highlights & Hints for Foundation Piecing

- Begin and end sewing at least two to three stitches beyond line you are sewing on, **Figure 21**.

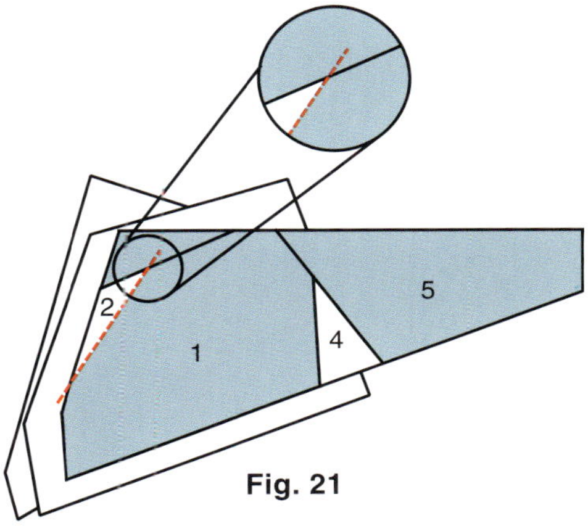

Fig. 21

- Don't worry if your stitching goes through a whole space and into another space, **Figure 22**; it will not interfere with adding subsequent pieces.

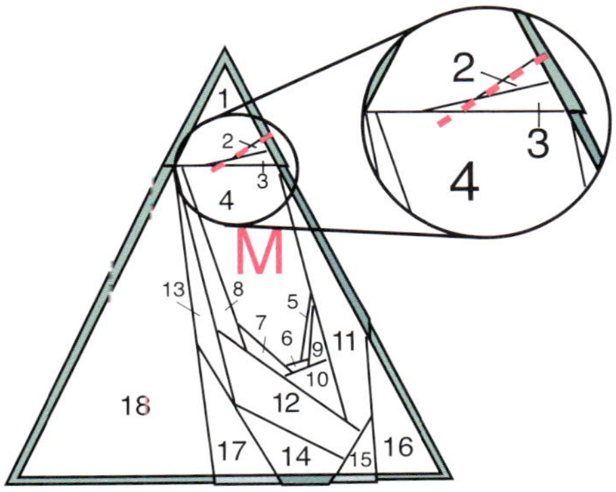

Fig. 22

- Finger-press or press with an iron after every seam. The little wooden "irons" found in quilt shops or catalogs work great.
- Use a short stitch, around 20 stitches per inch.
- Trim seam allowances to ⅛"–¼" (or smaller if necessary for small sections).
- Don't worry too much about grain line. Sewing to a foundation stabilizes the fabric and will prevent it from getting out of shape.
- When sewing spaces with points, it is easier to start sewing from the wide end toward the point, **Figure 23**.

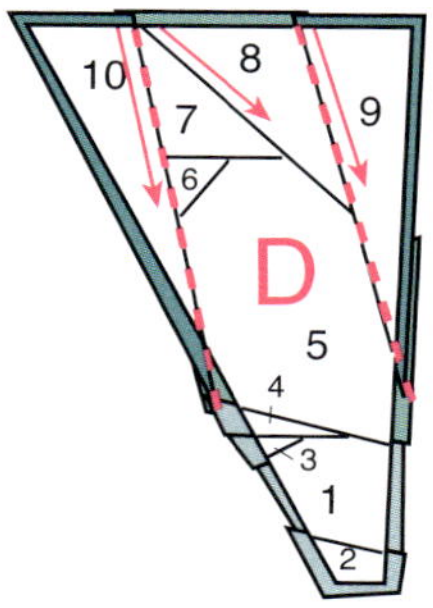

Fig. 23

- Directional prints are not recommended unless they are used only once in a block or are placed where they can be used easily in a consistent manner. If directional prints are placed randomly, the effect in the finished block may be undesirable.

Finishing the Quilt

Making the Quilt Top

Make the number of blocks necessary for your quilt top.

Lay out blocks in desired arrangement. Sew quilt blocks together in rows; press seams for rows in alternate directions. Sew rows together, matching seams.

To add borders, measure quilt top lengthwise; cut two border strips to that length and sew to sides of quilt. Measure quilt top crosswise, including borders just added; cut two border strips to that length. Sew to top and bottom edges of quilt top. Repeat for any additional borders. Remove paper foundations.

Layering the Quilt

There are many types of batting on the market. Use batting that is suitable for the use of your quilt. If making a wall hanging, choose a thin cotton or polyester batting. If making a bed quilt, you may want low-loft polyester batting for a little more thickness. Check the label to see the quilting requirements and follow those guidelines.

Use 100 percent cotton fabric for the backing of your quilt. For quilts wider than the 40"–44"-wide fabric, you will have to piece your backing unless you use the 90"–106"-wide fabrics that are currently available.

Cut backing and batting about 1"–2" larger on all sides than the quilt top. Place backing wrong side up and then smooth out batting on top. Center quilt top right side up on batting.

Baste layers together using one of the following techniques:

Fusible iron-on batting—Hobbs Heirloom Fusible Cotton Batting®, Fusible Batting™ by June Tailor, and Gold-Fuse by Mountain Mist® are wonderful new ways to hold the quilt layers together without using other time-consuming methods of basting.

Thread basting—Baste with long stitches, starting in center and sewing toward edges in a number of diagonal lines.

Safety pin basting—Pin through all layers at once, starting from center and working toward edges. Place pins no more than 4" apart, thinking of your quilt plan as you work to make certain pins avoid prospective quilting lines.

Quilt gun basting—Use the handy trigger tool (found in quilt and fabric stores) that pushes nylon tags through all layers of the quilt. Start in center and work randomly toward outside edges. Place tags about 4" apart. You can sew right over the tags and then easily remove them by cutting off with a pair of scissors.

Spray or heat-set basting—Use one of the spray adhesives currently on the market, following manufacturer's directions.

Quilting

If you have never used a sewing machine for quilting, you might want to read more about the technique. *Learn to Machine Quilt in Just One Weekend* (ASN #4186), by Marti Michell, is an excellent introduction to machine quilting. This book is available at your local quilt or fabric store, or write the publisher for a list of sources.

You do not need a special machine for quilting. Just make sure your machine is oiled and in good working condition. An even-feed foot is a good investment if you are going to machine-quilt, since it is designed to feed the top and bottom layers of the quilt through the machine evenly. Use fine transparent nylon thread in the top and regular sewing thread in the bobbin.

To **quilt-in-the-ditch** of a seam (this is actually stitching in the space between two pieces of fabric that have been sewn together), use your fingers to pull blocks or pieces apart slightly and machine-stitch right between the two pieces. Try to keep stitching to the side of the seam that does not have the bulk of the seam allowance under it. When you have finished stitching, the quilting will be practically hidden in the seam.

Free-form machine quilting is done with a darning foot and the feed dogs down on your sewing machine. It can be used to quilt around a design or to quilt a motif. Free-form machine quilting takes practice to master, because you are controlling the movement of the quilt under the needle rather than the machine moving the quilt. With free-form machine quilting, you can quilt in any direction: up and down, side to side and even in circles, without pivoting the quilt around the needle.

Attaching the Binding

Trim backing and batting even with quilt top. Cut enough 2½"-wide strips to go around all four sides of the quilt, plus 6". Join strips end-to-end with diagonal seams; trim corners, **Figure 24**.

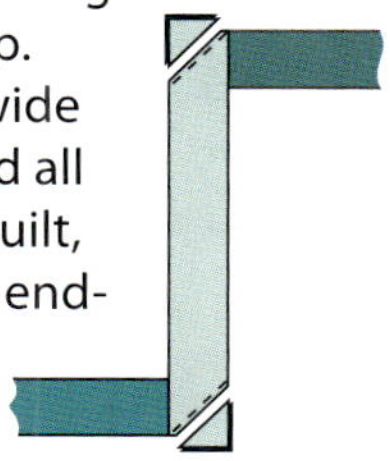

Fig. 24

Press seams open. Cut one end of strip at a 45-degree angle, and then press under ¼", **Figure 25**.

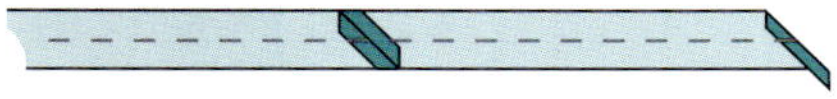

Fig. 25

Press entire strip in half lengthwise, wrong sides together, **Figure 26**.

Fig. 26

On right side of quilt, position binding in middle of one side, aligning raw edges. Sew binding to quilt using ¼" seam, beginning about an inch below folded end of binding. At corner, stop ¼" from edge of quilt and backstitch, **Figure 27**.

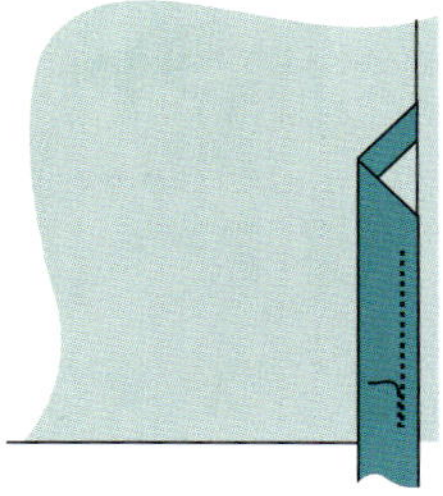

Fig. 27

Fold binding away from quilt at a 45-degree angle. Fold binding back on itself so fold is on quilt edge and raw edges are aligned with adjacent side of quilt, **Figure 28**. Begin sewing at quilt edge.

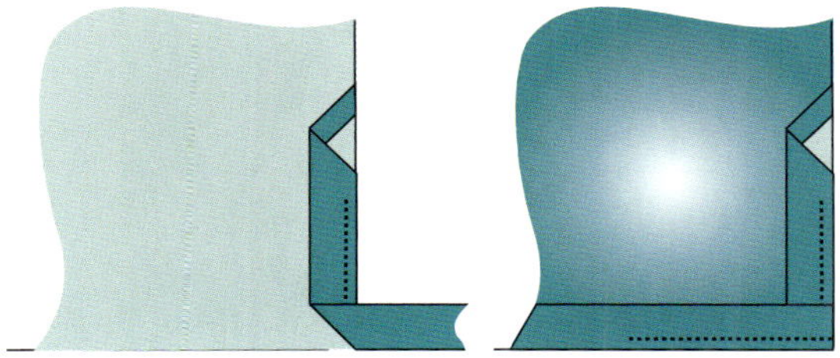

Fig. 28

Continue in the same manner around remaining sides of quilt. To finish, stop about two inches away from starting point. Trim excess binding, and then tuck inside folded end, **Figure 29**. Finish line of stitching.

Fold binding to back of quilt so seam line is covered; blindstitch in place.

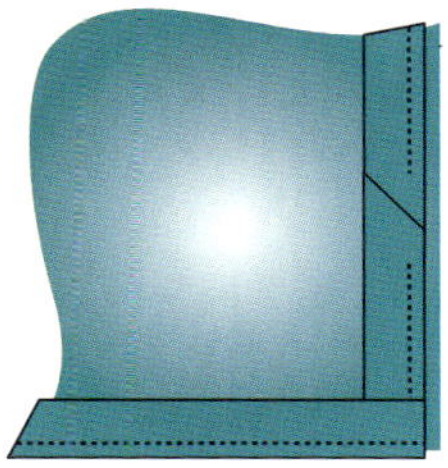

Fig. 29

The Finishing Touch

After your quilt is finished, always sign and date it. A label can be cross-stitched, embroidered or even written with a permanent marking pen. To make decorative labels in a hurry, *Iron-on Transfers for Quilt Labels* (ASN #4188) and *Foundation-Pieced Quilt Labels* (ASN #4196) provide many patterns for fun and unique quilt labels. Hand-stitch to back of quilt.

How to Make a Tassel

Cut an index card or piece of cardboard 3 inches high.

Cut a 3-inch piece of gold metallic thread and lay it along the top of the cardboard. Wrap the thread from the spool around the cardboard from bottom to top 50 times, ending at the bottom. Clip the spool thread.

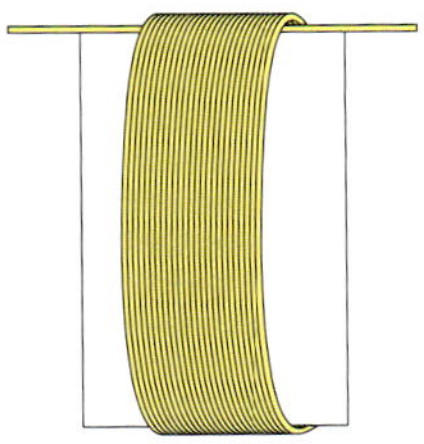

Fig. 1

Grasping the single thread at both ends, slide the wrapped threads off the cardboard.

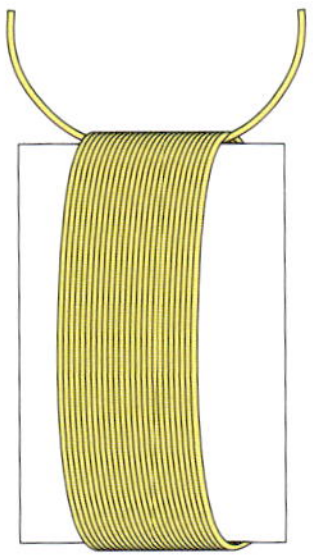

Fig. 2

Tie a knot with the single thread to secure all the wrapped threads. Clip the ends of the knotted thread close to the knot.

Cut a 12-inch piece of thread and wrap it five times around the tassel, about ¼ inch below the knot. This pulls all the threads together and forms the head of the tassel.

Fig. 3

Use this thread to sew the tassel to the quilt block.

Trim the tassel to 1⅛ inches.

Fire Engine

Special note: *Attach 3 white with silver tone ½-inch buttons on tires for hubcaps.*

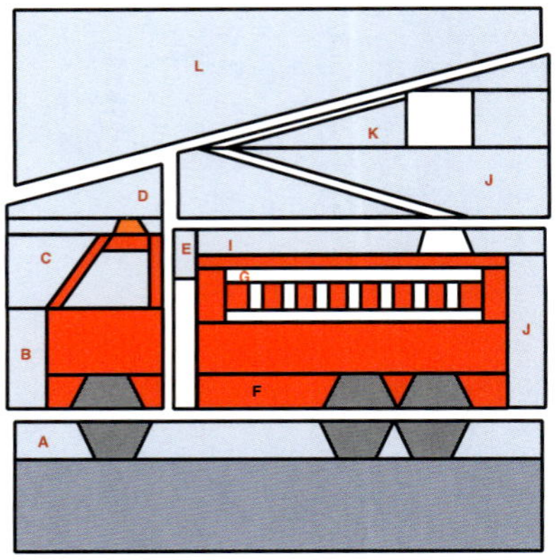

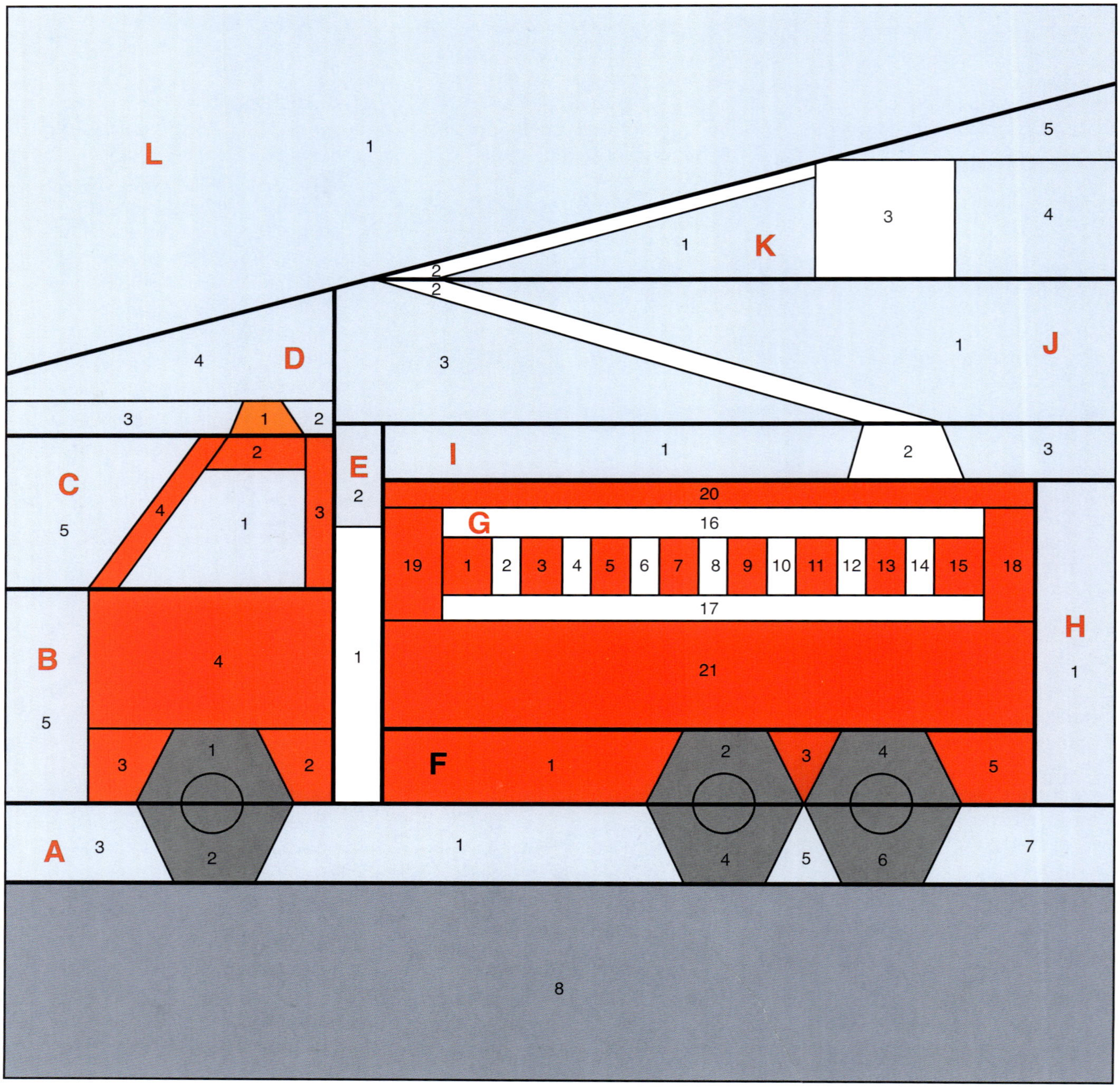

Fire Engine

American School of Needlework • Berne, Indiana 46711 • DRGnetwork.com

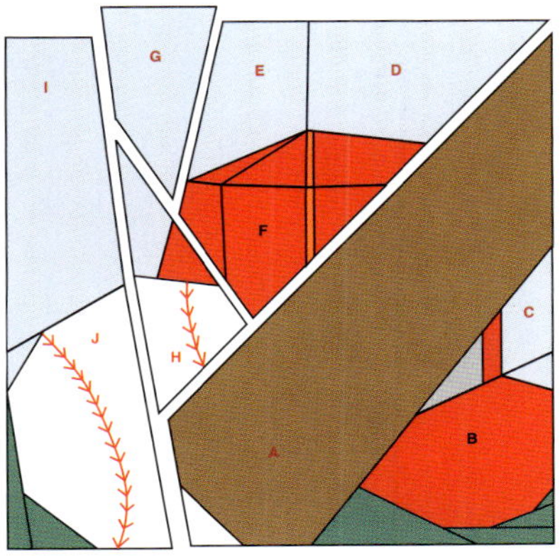

Baseball, Bat & Cap

Special notes: *Machine-stitch detail on cap visor and top of cap; draw baseball seams with permanent fine-line marker.*

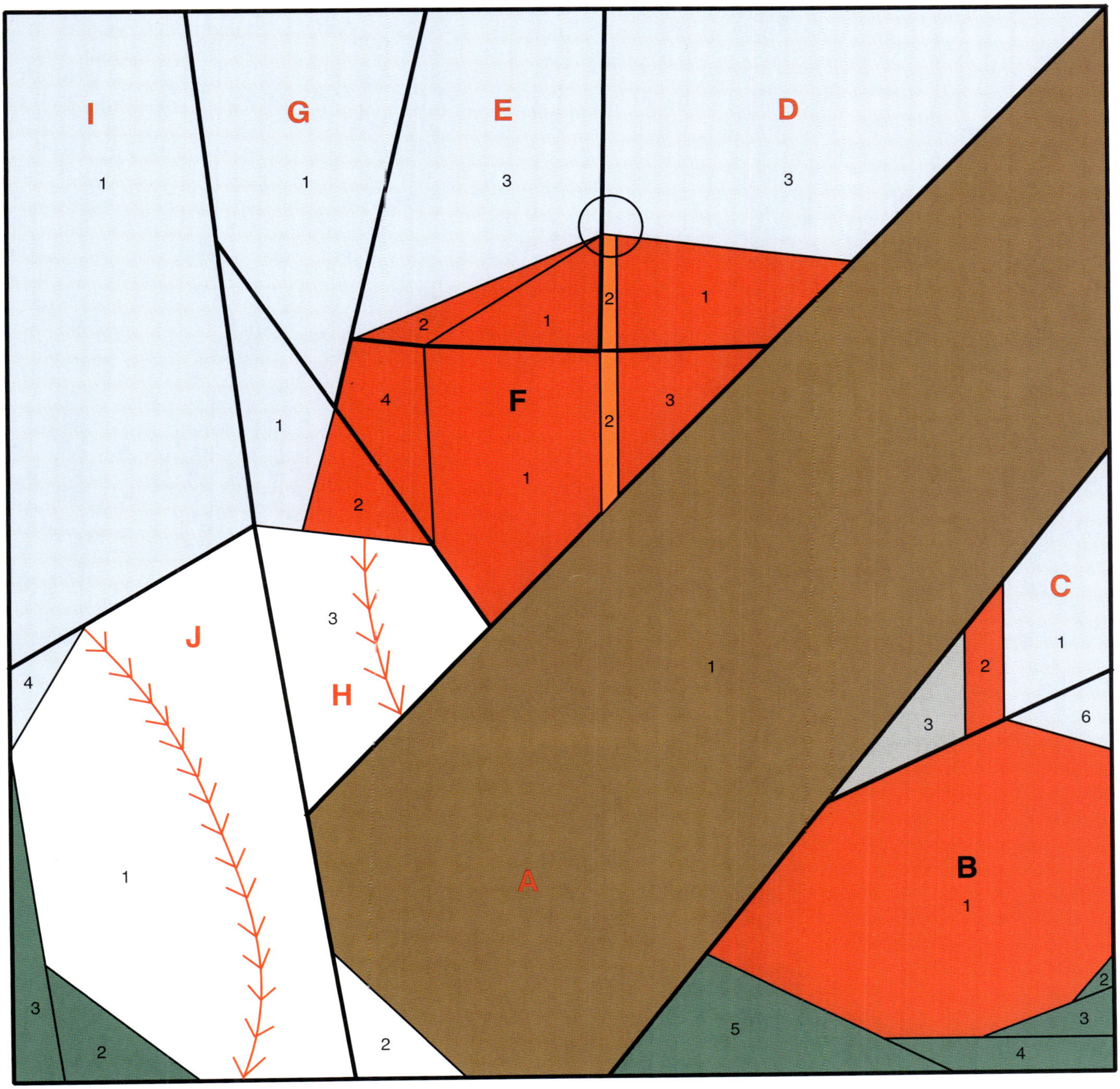

Baseball, Bat & Cap

Soccer Ball

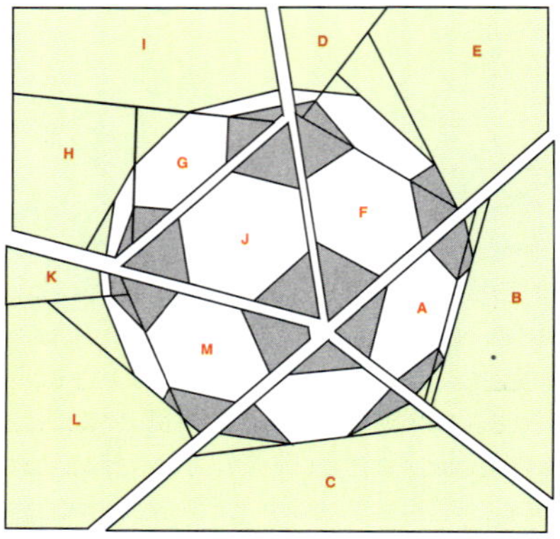

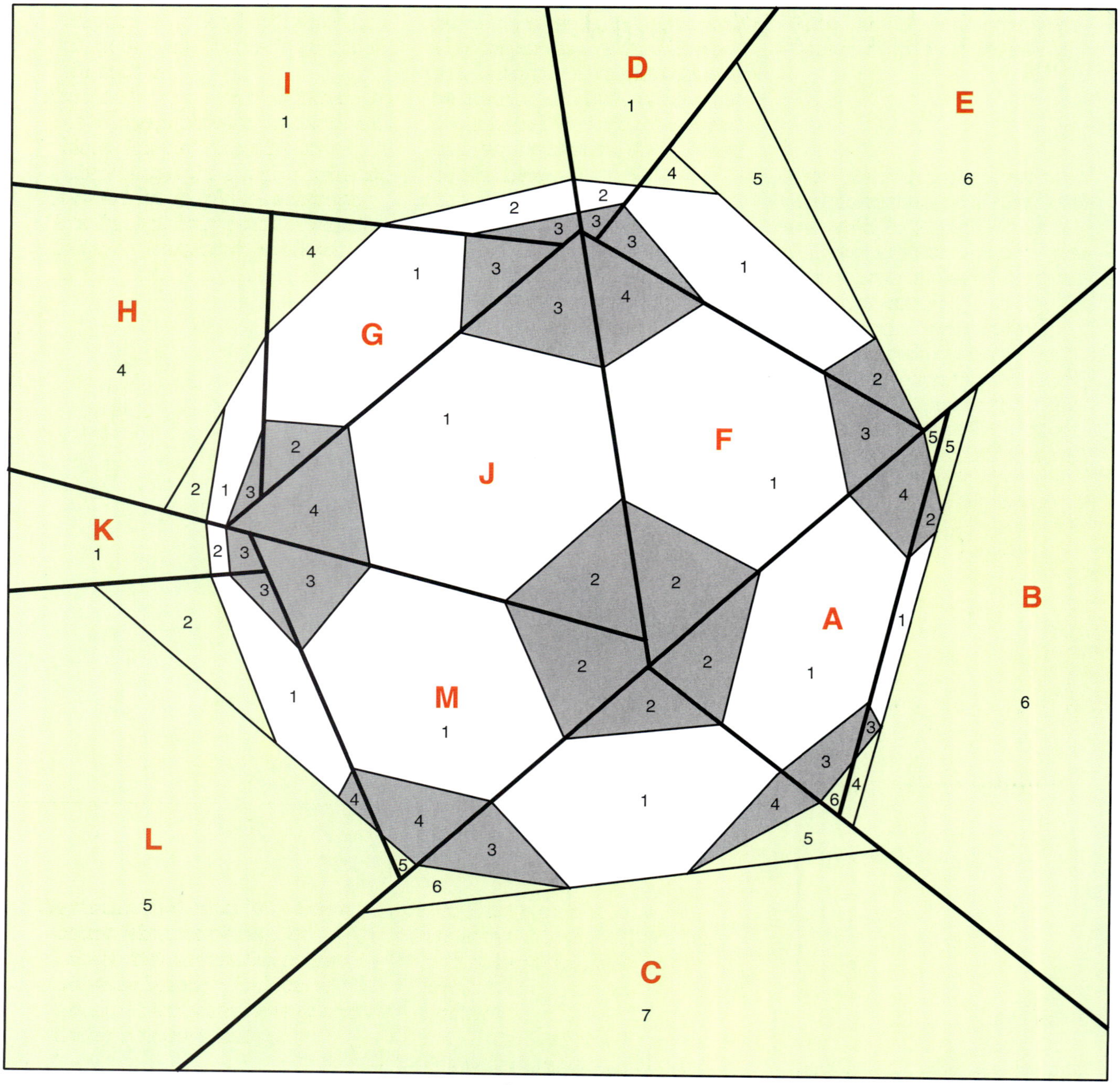

Soccer Ball

American School of Needlework • Berne, Indiana 46711 • DRGnetwork.com

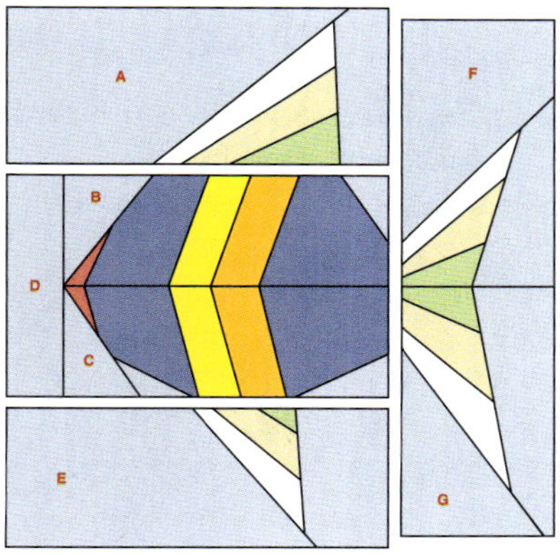

Fish

Special notes: *Attach 1 black swirl ⅜-inch button for fish eye and 3 iridescent clear 5⁄16-inch buttons for bubbles.*

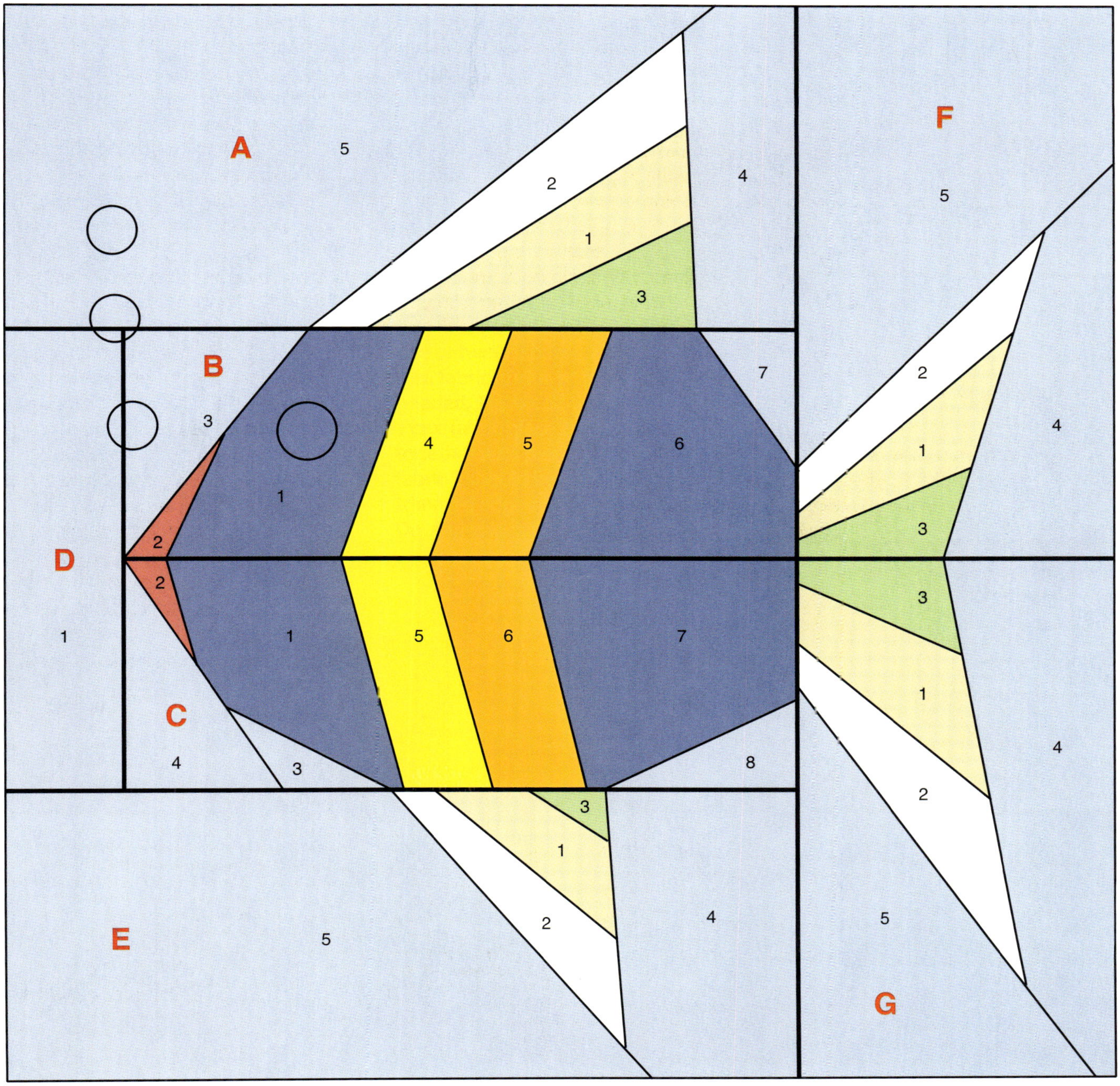

Fish

Pinwheels

Special note: *Attach 4 gold tone 7/16-inch buttons to centers of pinwheels.*

Pinwheels

American School of Needlework • Berne, Indiana 46711 • DRGnetwork.com

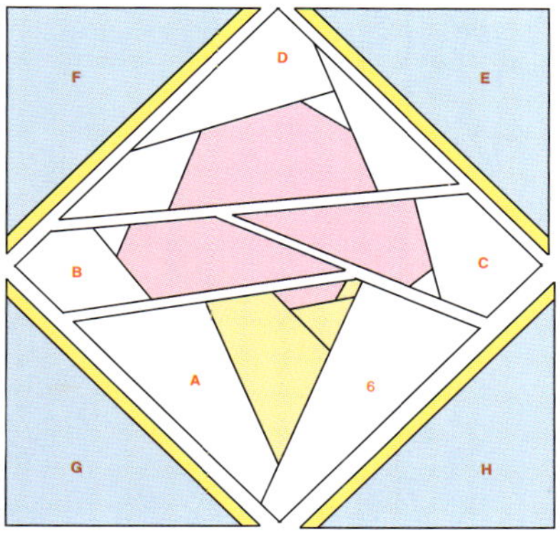

Ice-Cream Cone

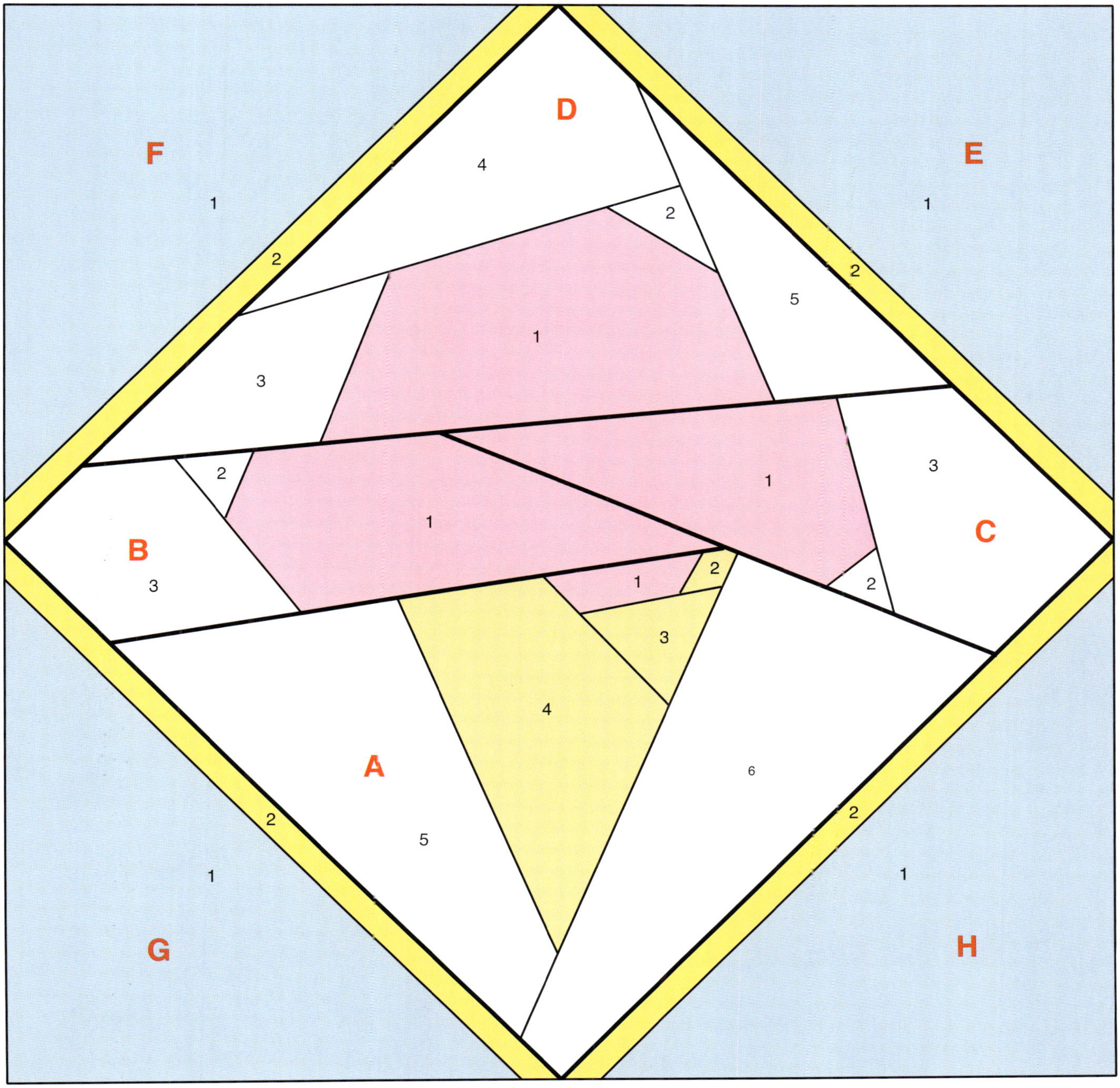

Ice-Cream Cone

Flip-Flops

Special notes: *Attach 2 white 1¾-inch fabric flowers and 2 yellow ½-inch buttons to center of flip-flops.*

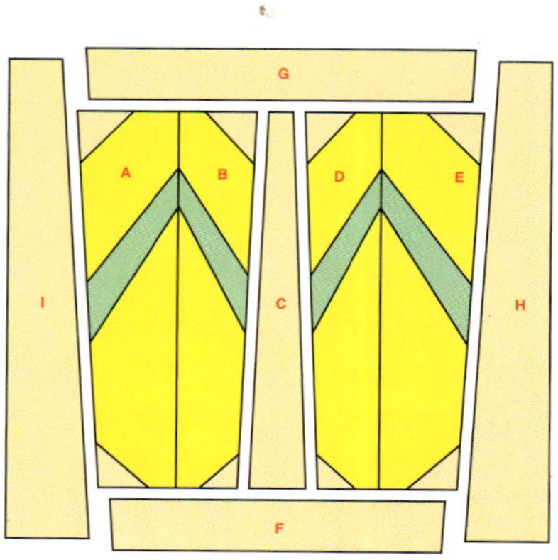

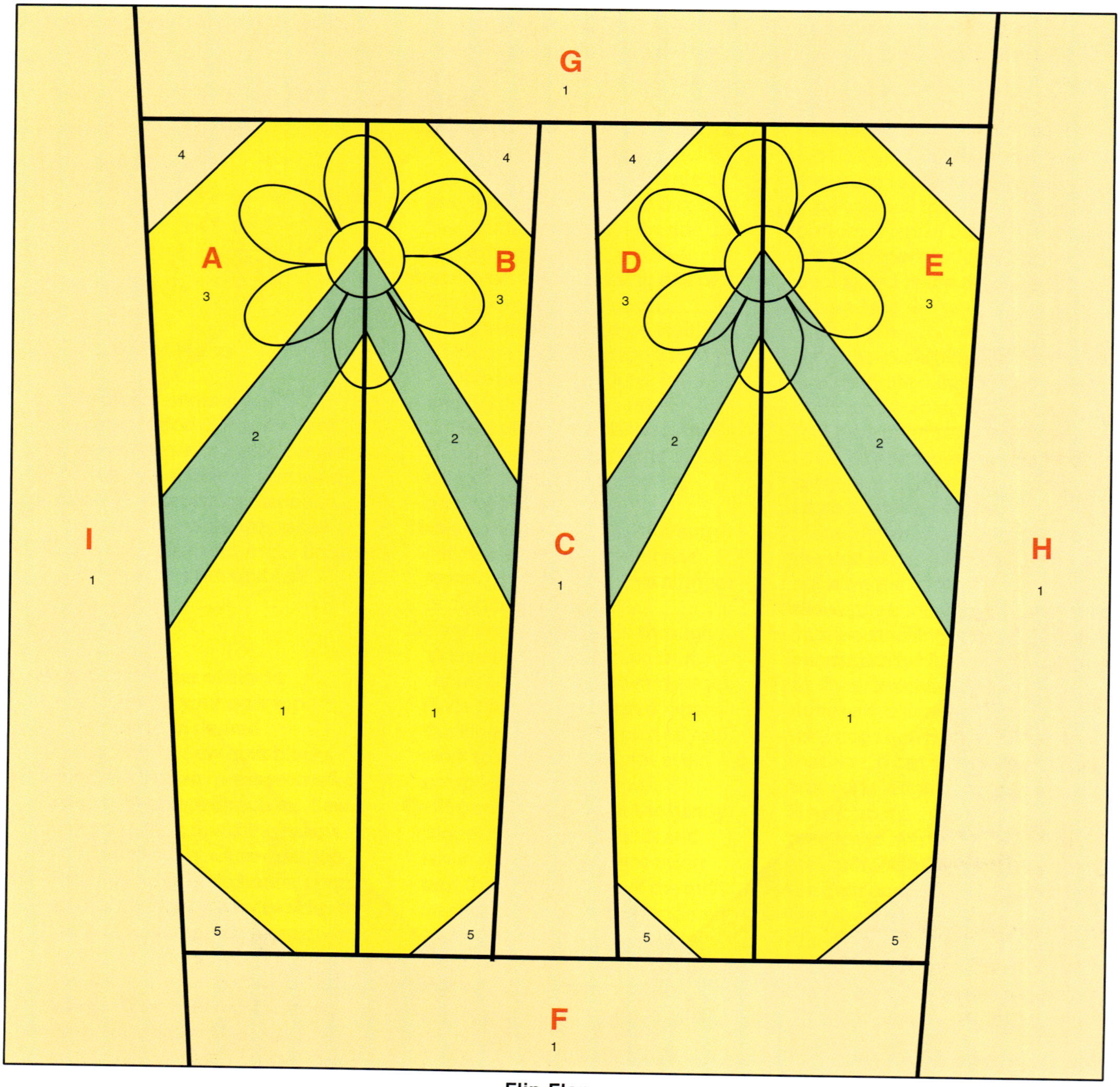

Flip-Flops

American School of Needlework • Berne, Indiana 46711 • DRGnetwork.com

Race Car

Special notes: *Attach 2 silver tone ⅝-inch buttons and 2 white pearl ⅜-inch buttons to tires for hubcaps.*

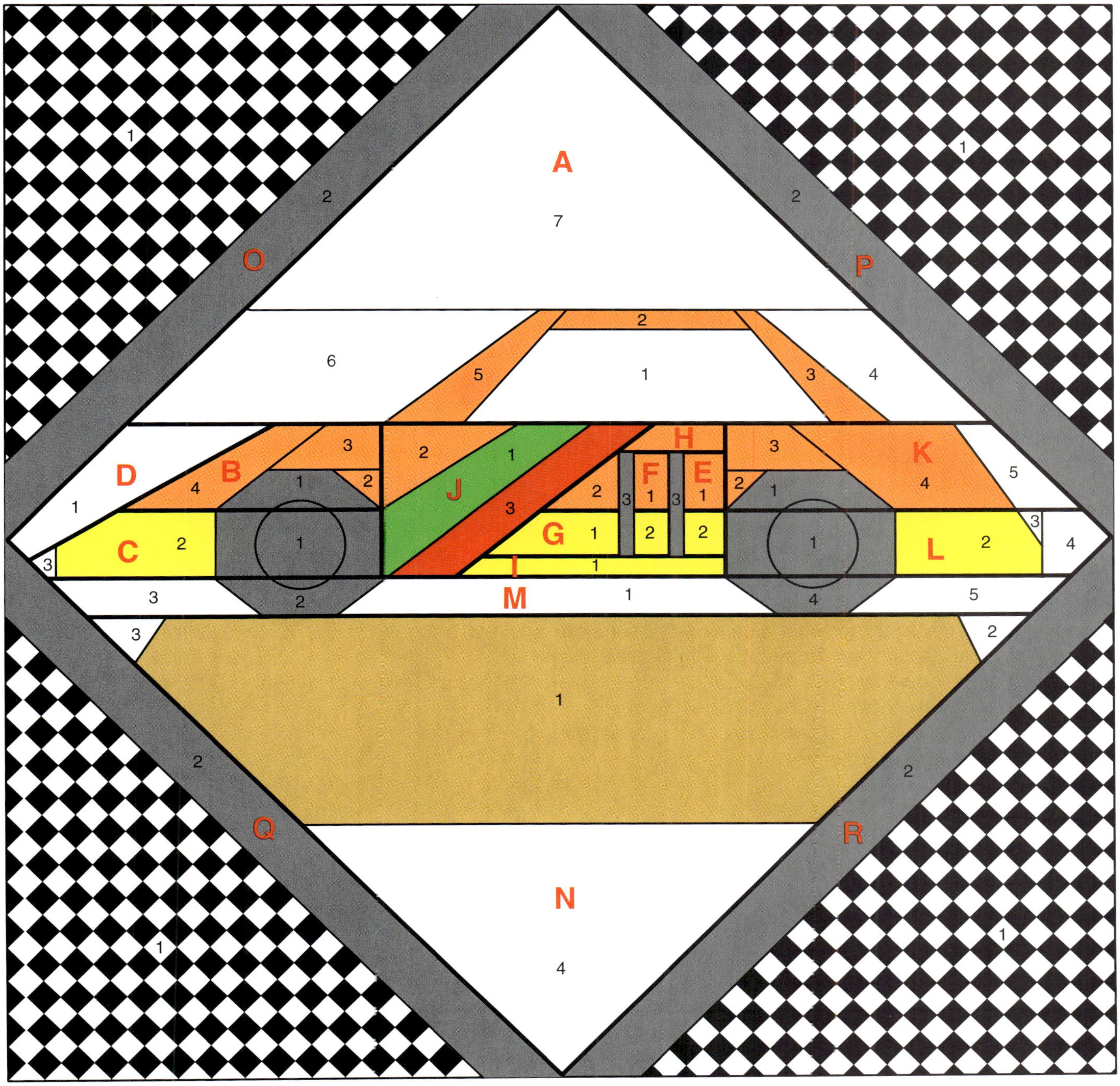

Race Car

Stars

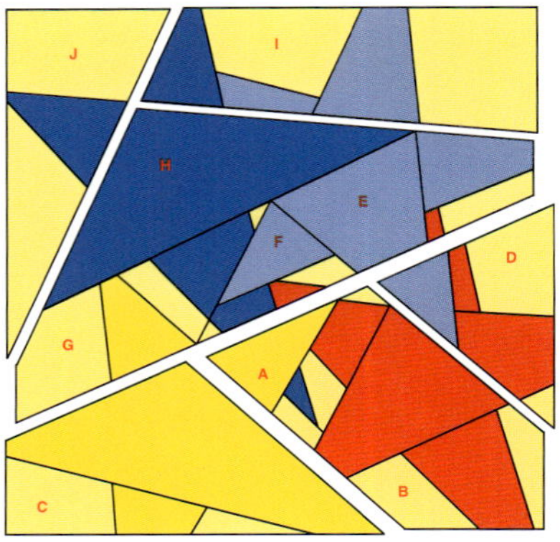

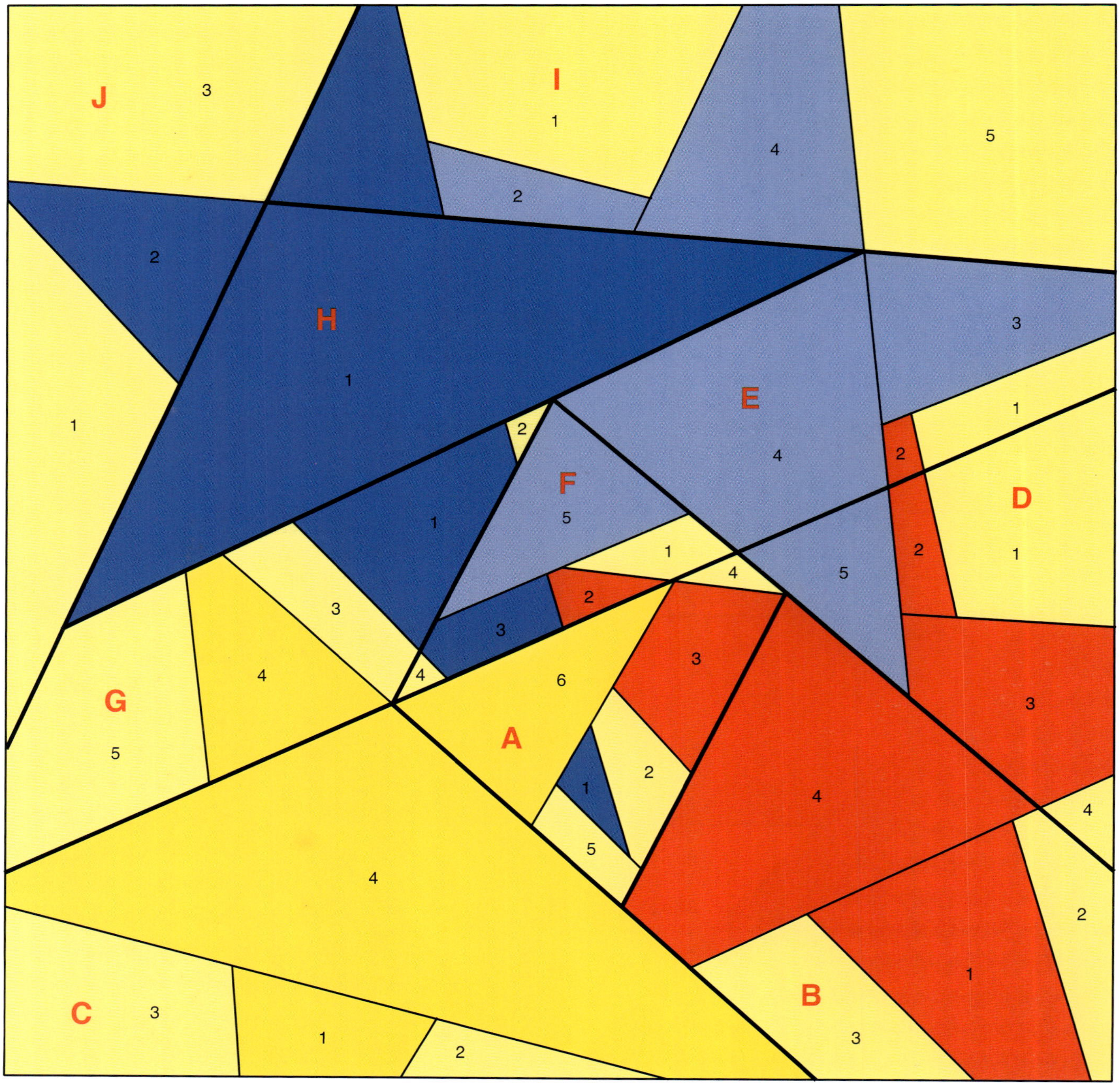

Stars

American School of Needlework • Berne, Indiana 46711 • DRGnetwork.com

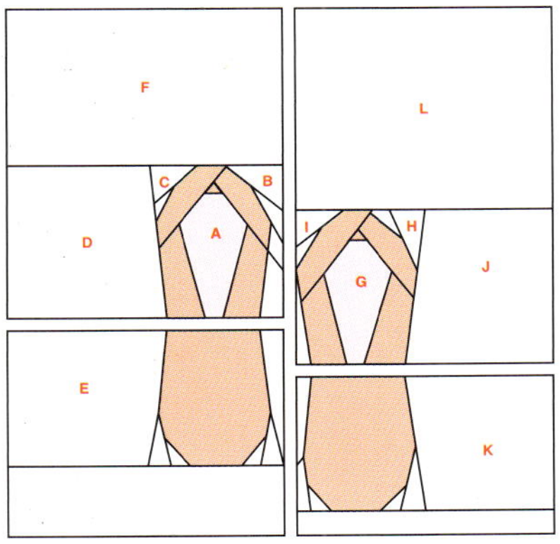

Ballerina Slippers

Special note: *Attach 4 (8-inch) lengths of pink ⅛-inch satin ribbon for ties.*

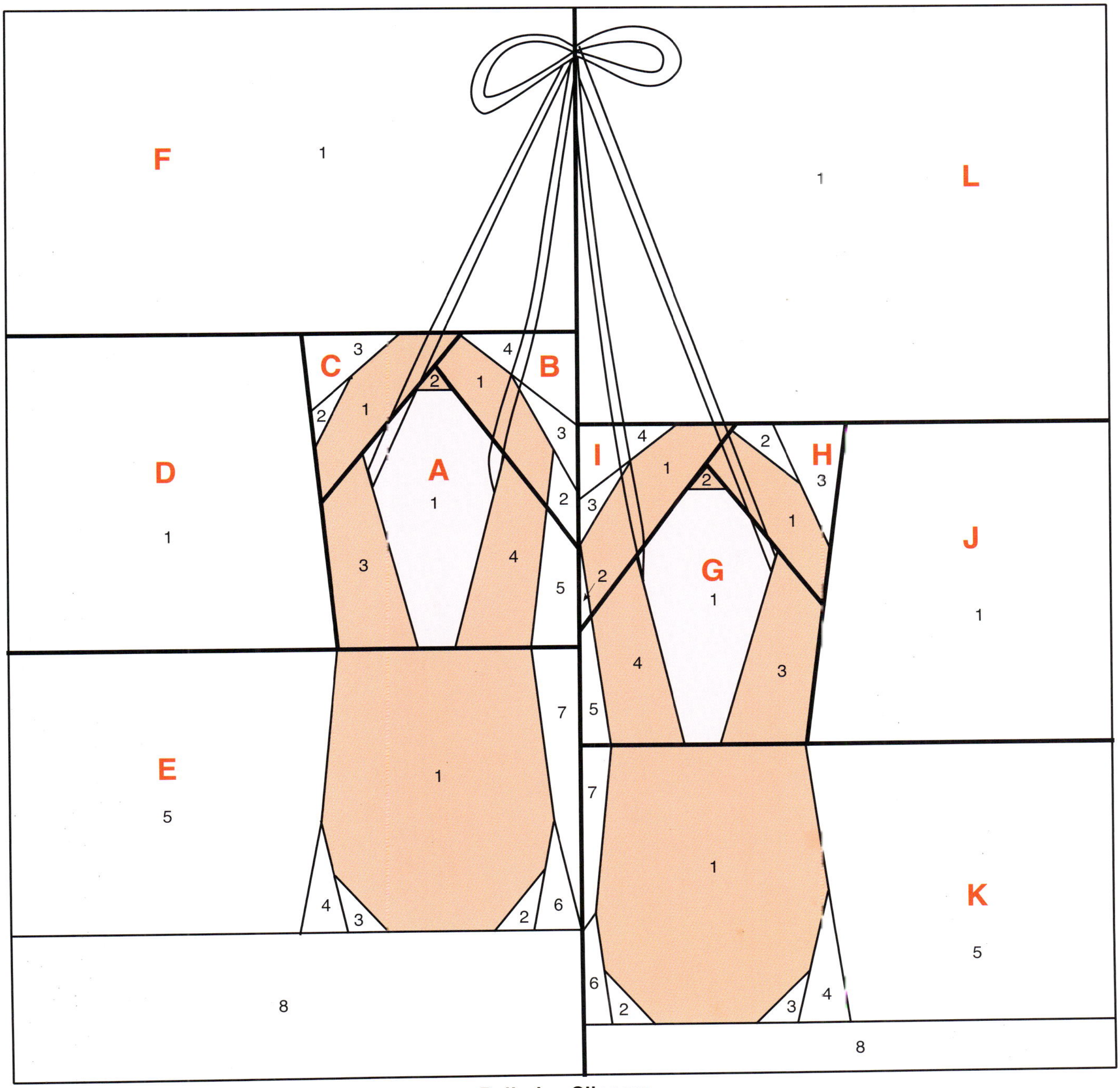

Ballerina Slippers

Kites

Special notes: *Machine- or hand-stitch kite strings; attach fabric scraps to kite tails.*

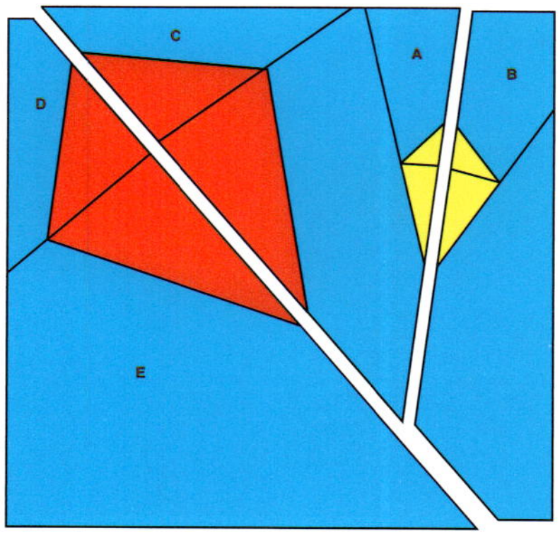

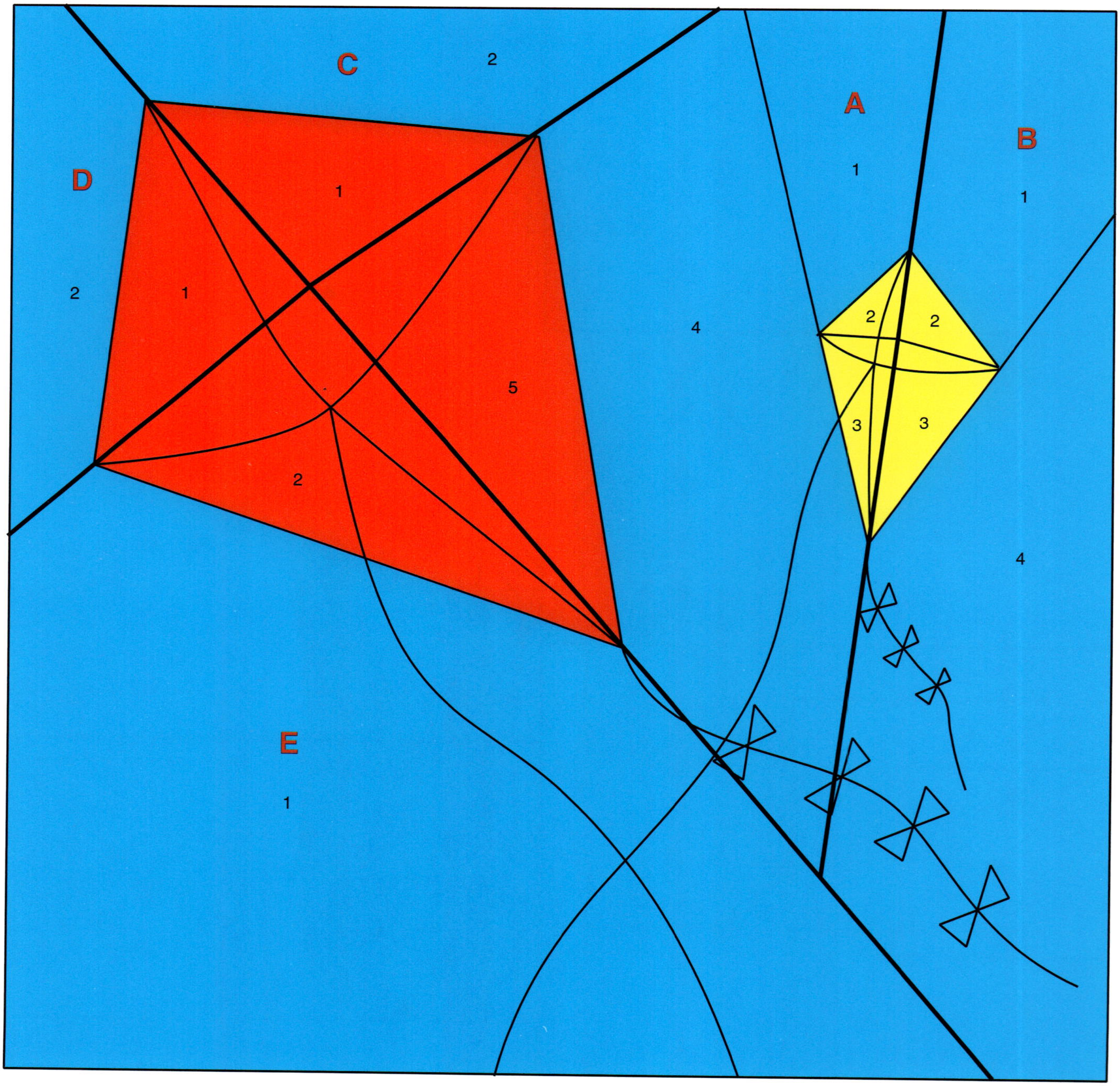

Kites

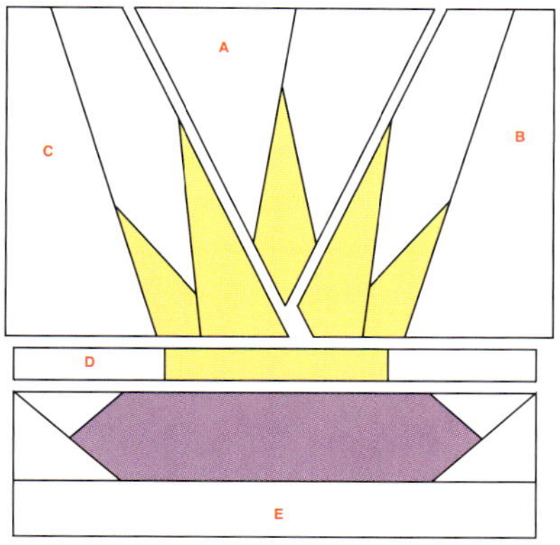

Princess Crown

Special notes: *Attach 5 (5mm) Rectangle Amethyst Metal Sliders (Crystal Innovations™ Sku#346640) to crown band, 1 (18 x 13mm) oval amber acrylic jewel to center of crown, 5 (7mm) clear round acrylic jewels to crown points, and 2 gold tassels (Coats metallic embroidery thread, Art#D79, gold, color #801) to pillow. (See How to Make A Tassel, page 7.)*

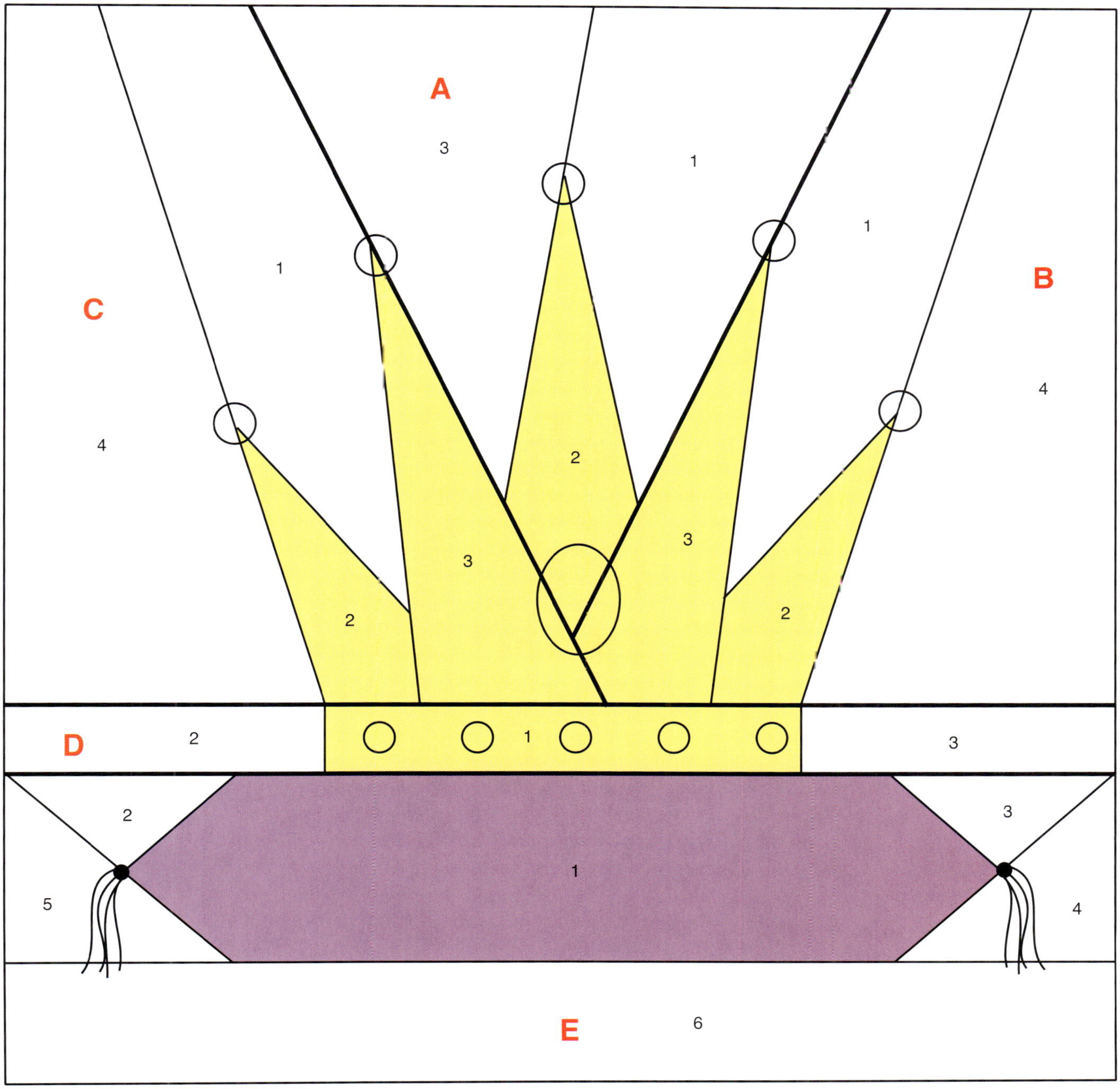

Princess Crown

Balloons

Special note: *Machine- or hand-stitch balloon strings.*

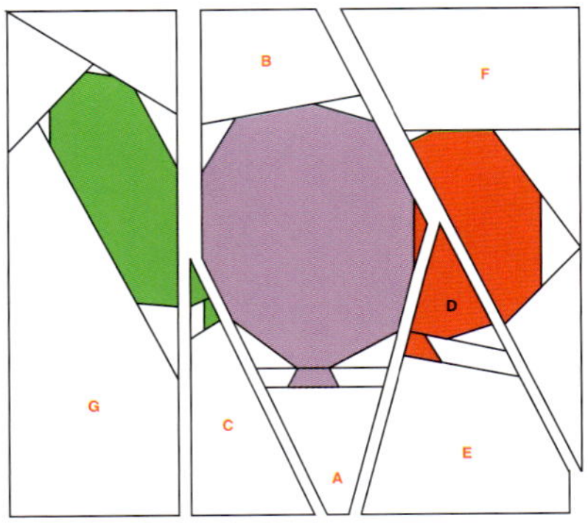

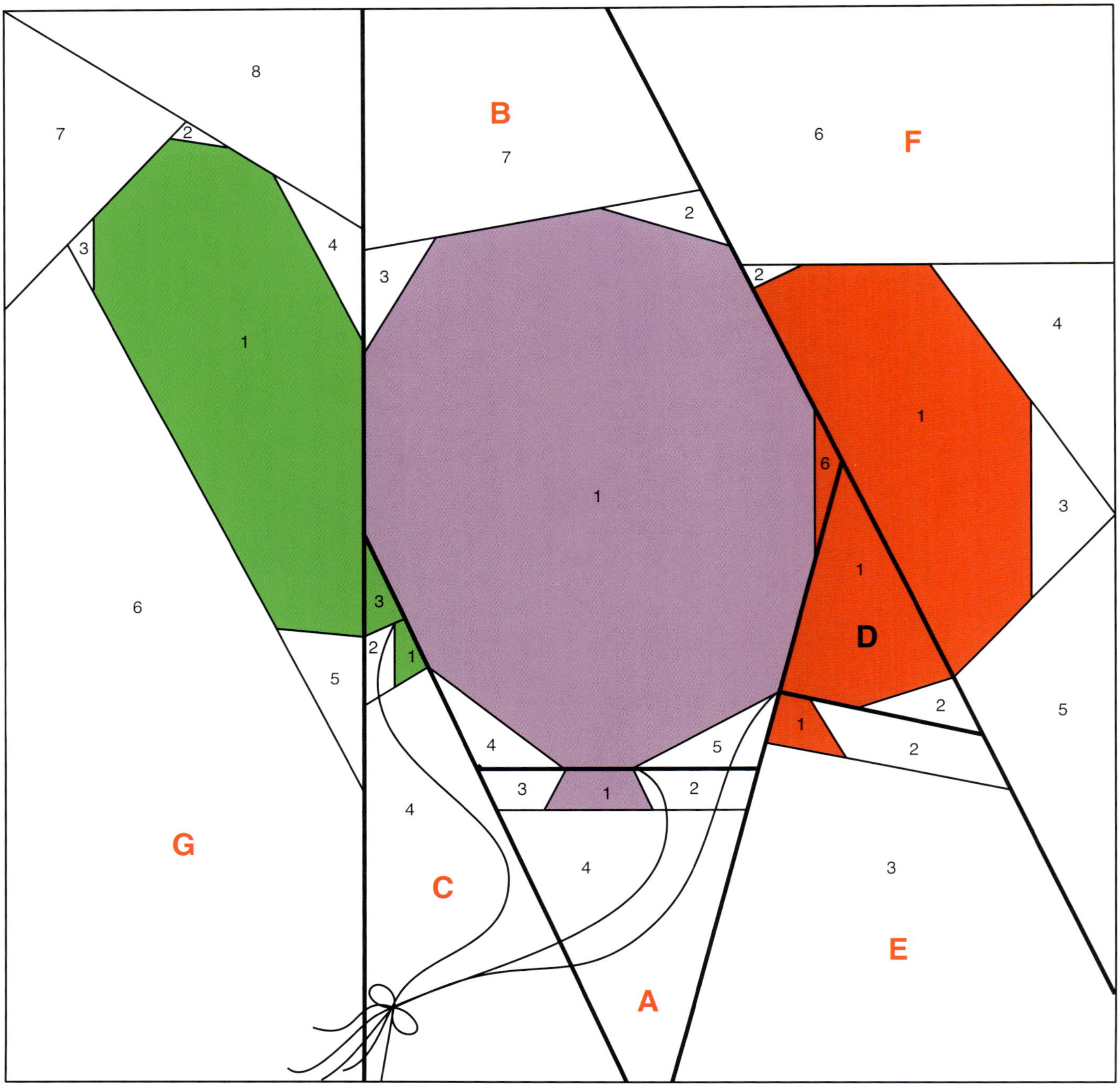

Balloons

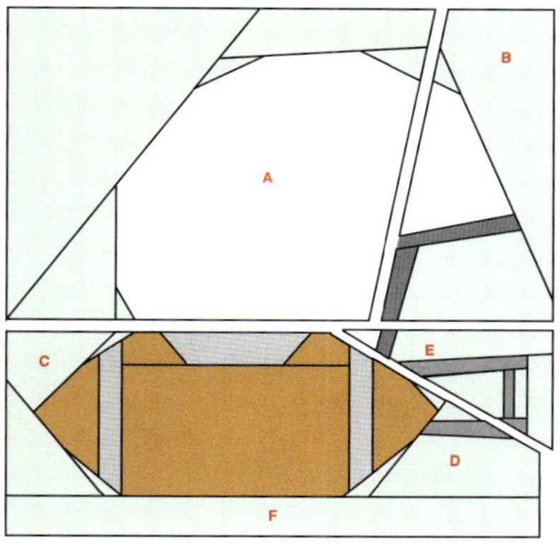

Football & Helmet

***Special note:** Draw football laces with permanent fine-line marker.*

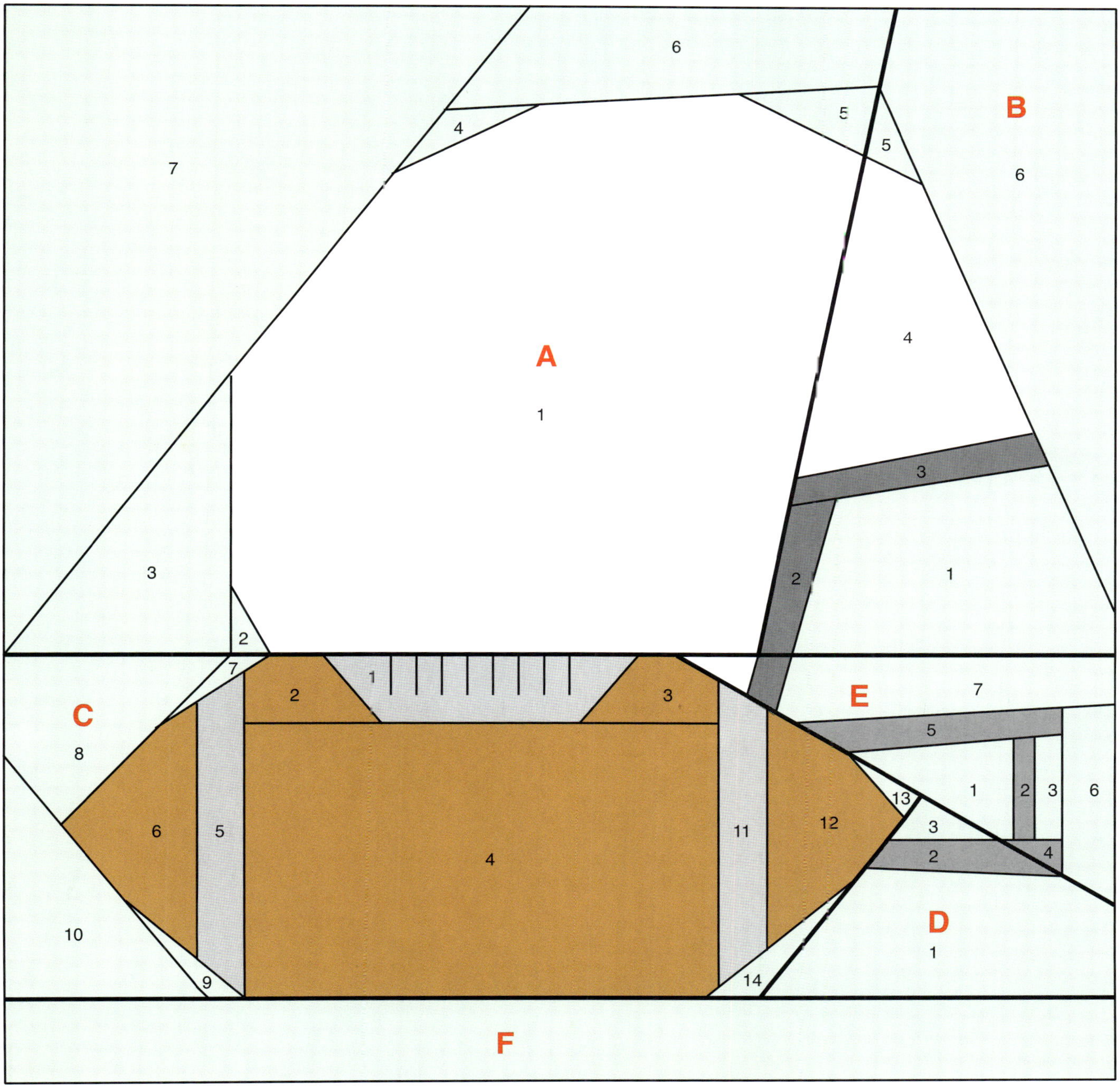

Football & Helmet

Man in the Moon

***Special note**: Draw face with permanent fine-line marker.*

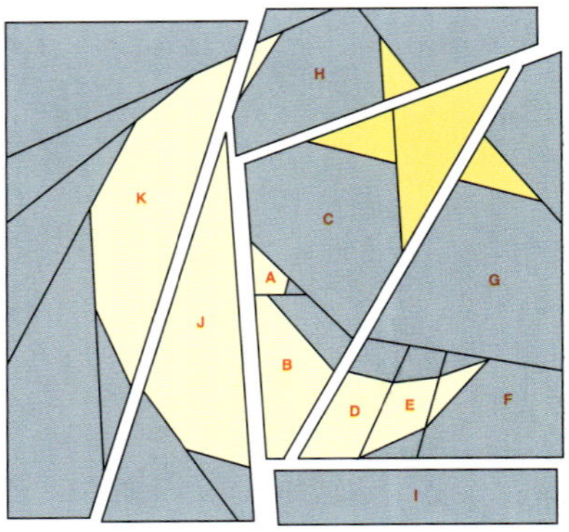

Man in the Moon

 American School of Needlework • Berne, Indiana 46711 • DRGnetwork.com

Sleeping Cat

Special note: *Draw face and paw with permanent fine-line marker.*

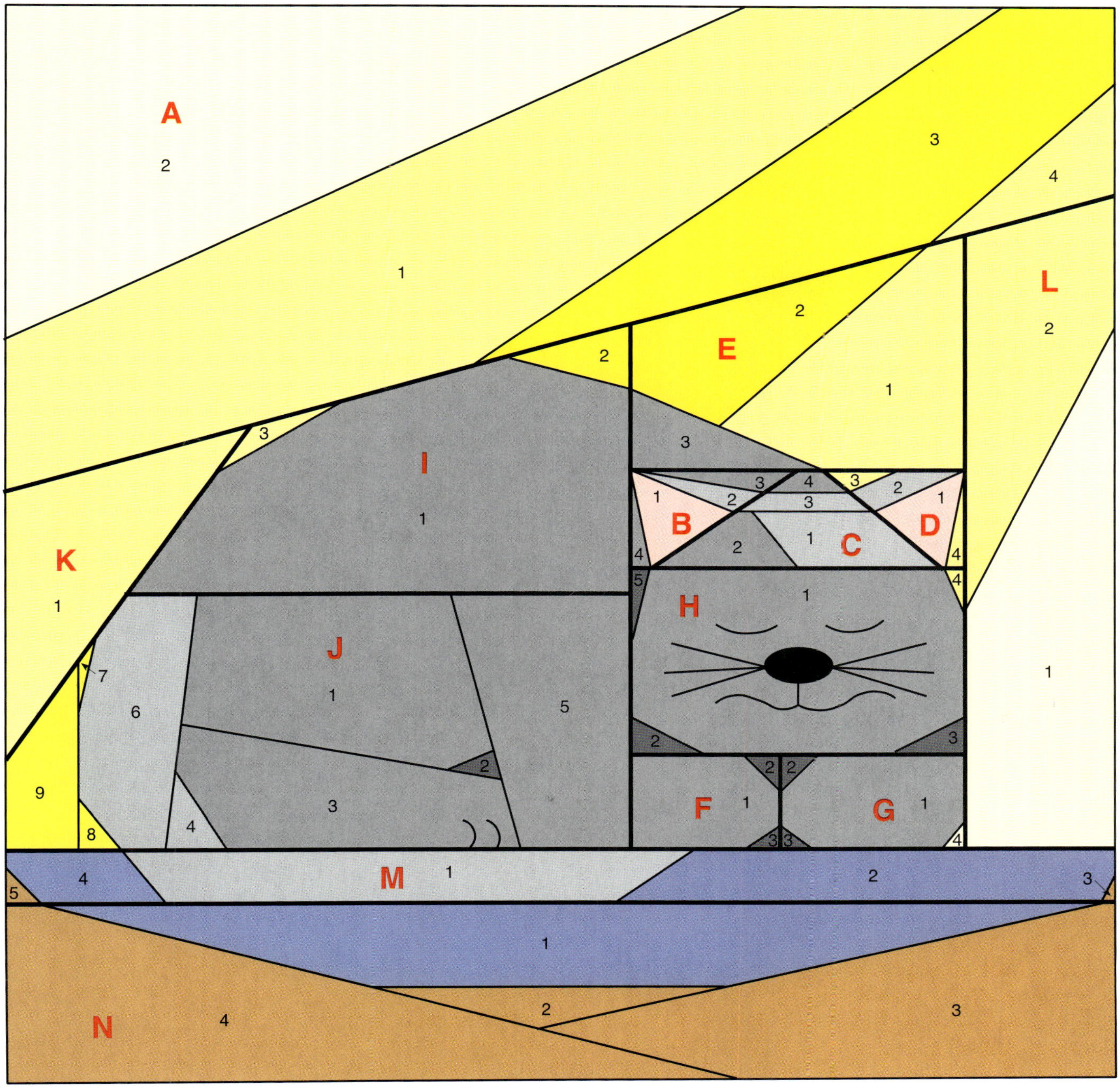

Sleeping Cat

Heart

A
B
D
C

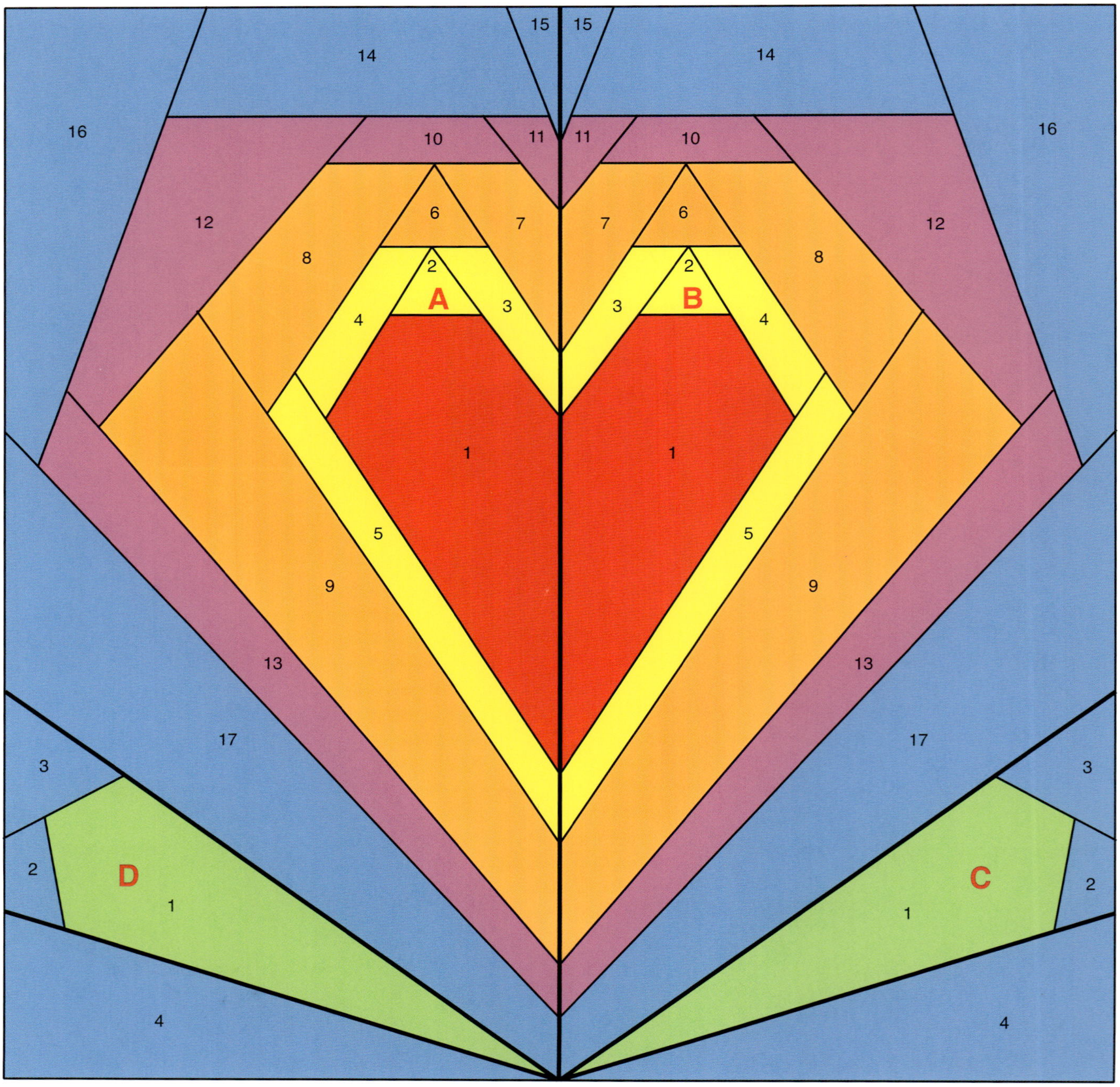
15
15
14
14
16
16
10
11
11
10
12
6
7
7
6
12
8
2
2
8
A
3
3
B
4
4
1
1
5
5
9
9
13
13
17
17
3
3
2
D
1
C
2
1
4
4

Heart

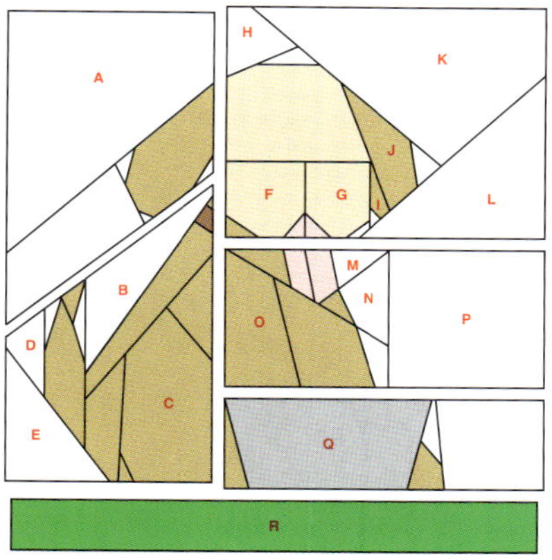

Puppy

Special note: *Draw nose, eyes and eyebrows with permanent fine-line marker.*

Puppy

Sand Pail & Shovel

Special note: *Attach red ⅜-inch button on handle.*

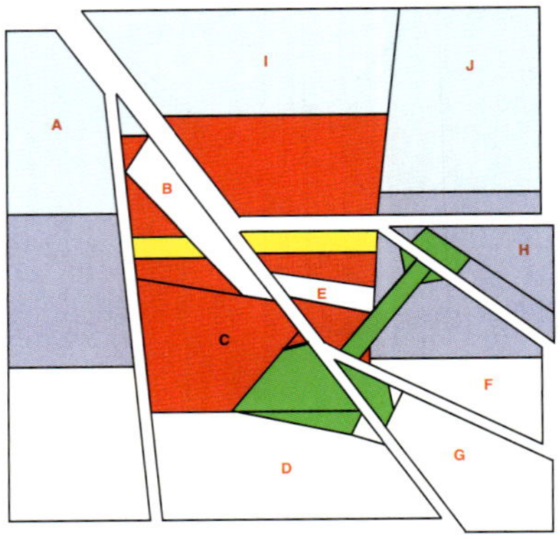

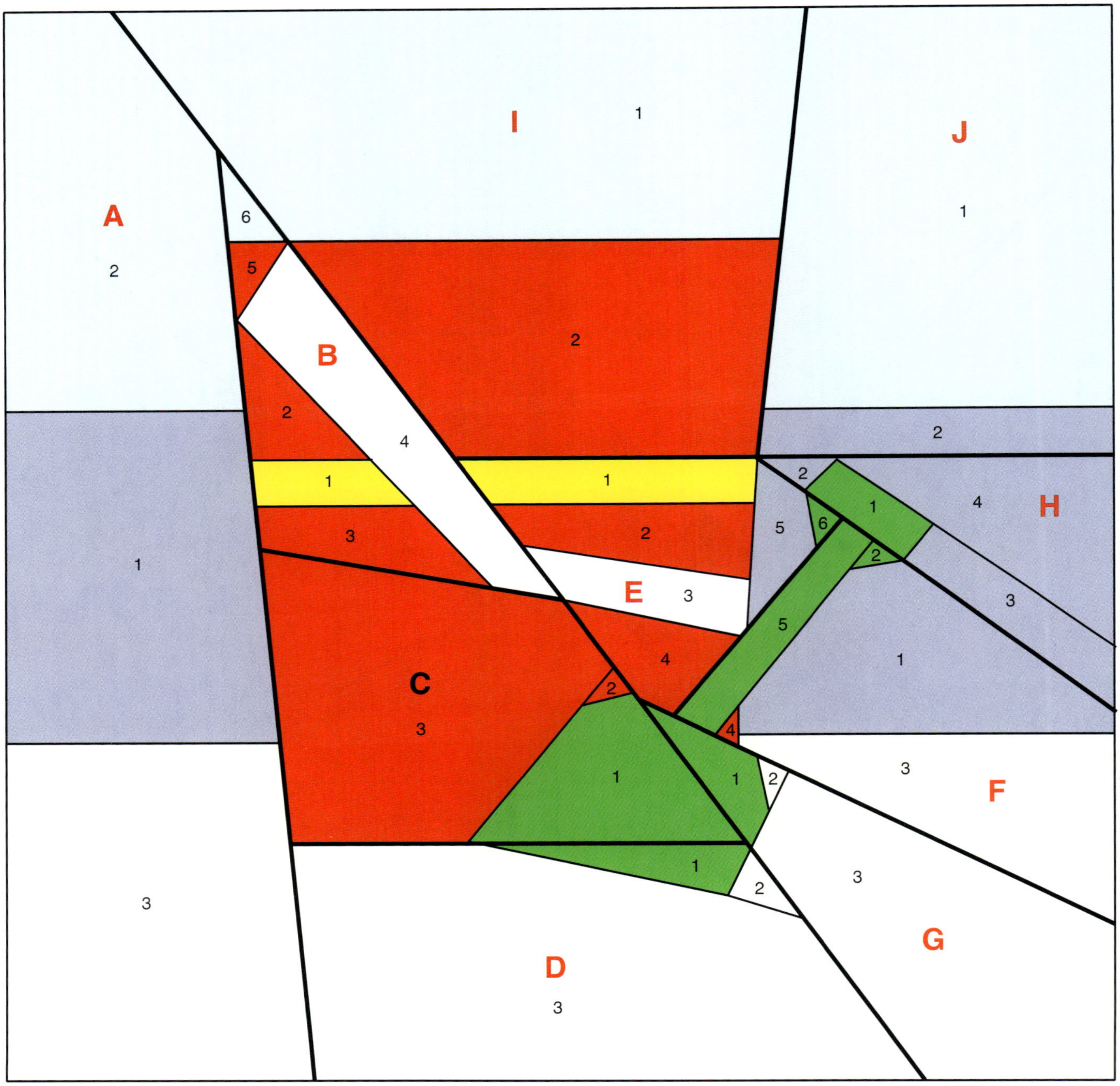

Sand Pail & Shovel

Sun

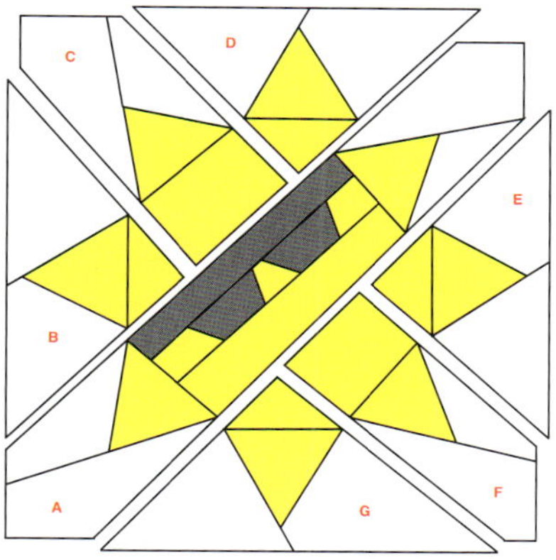
C
D
E
B
A
G
F

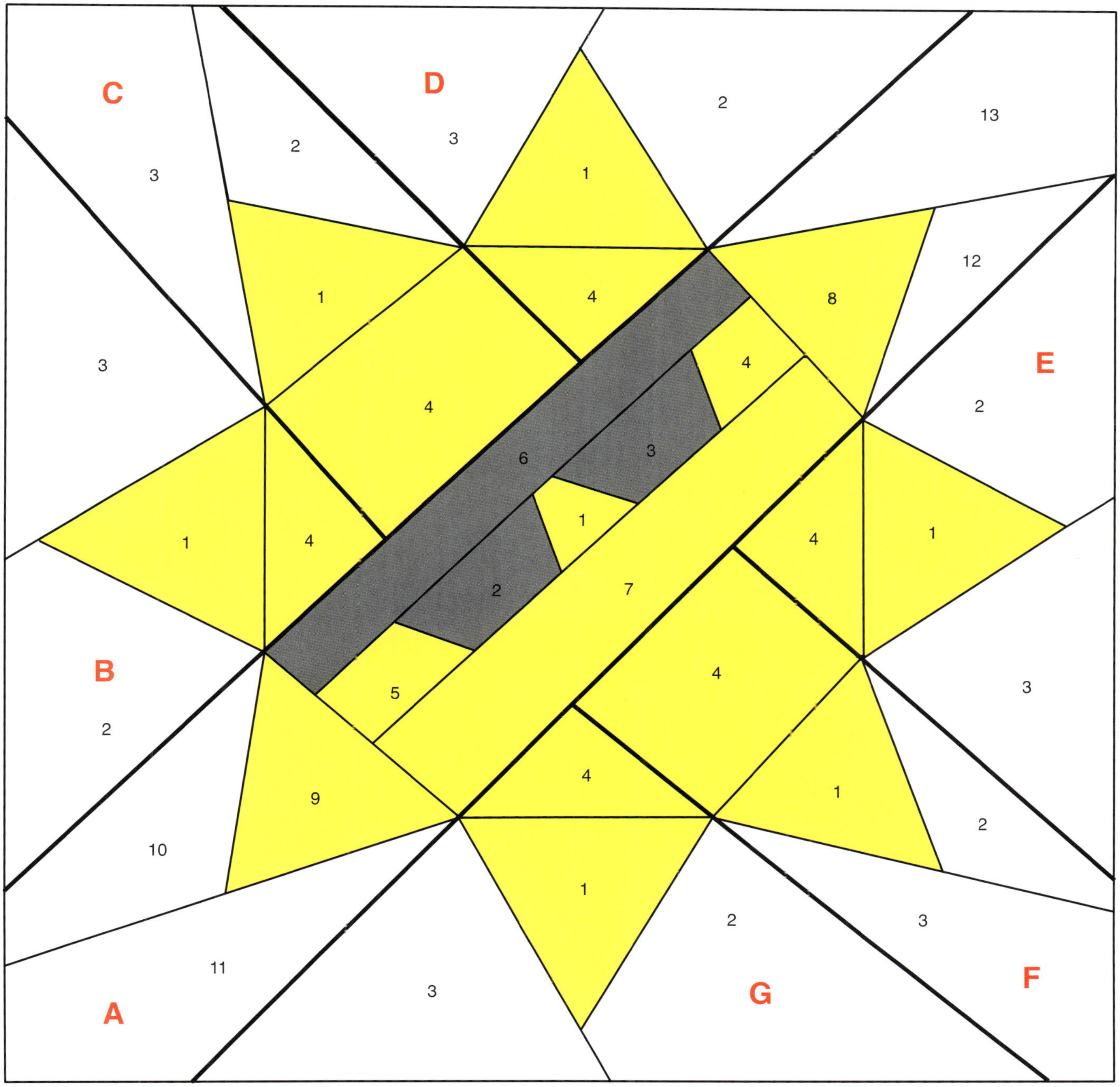
C
D
2
13
3
2
3
1
12
1
4
8
E
3
4
4
2
6
3
1
1
4
4
1
2
7
B
5
4
3
2
9
4
1
2
10
1
2
3
11
3
A
G
F

Sun

Butterfly

Special note: *Machine- or hand-stitch antennae.*

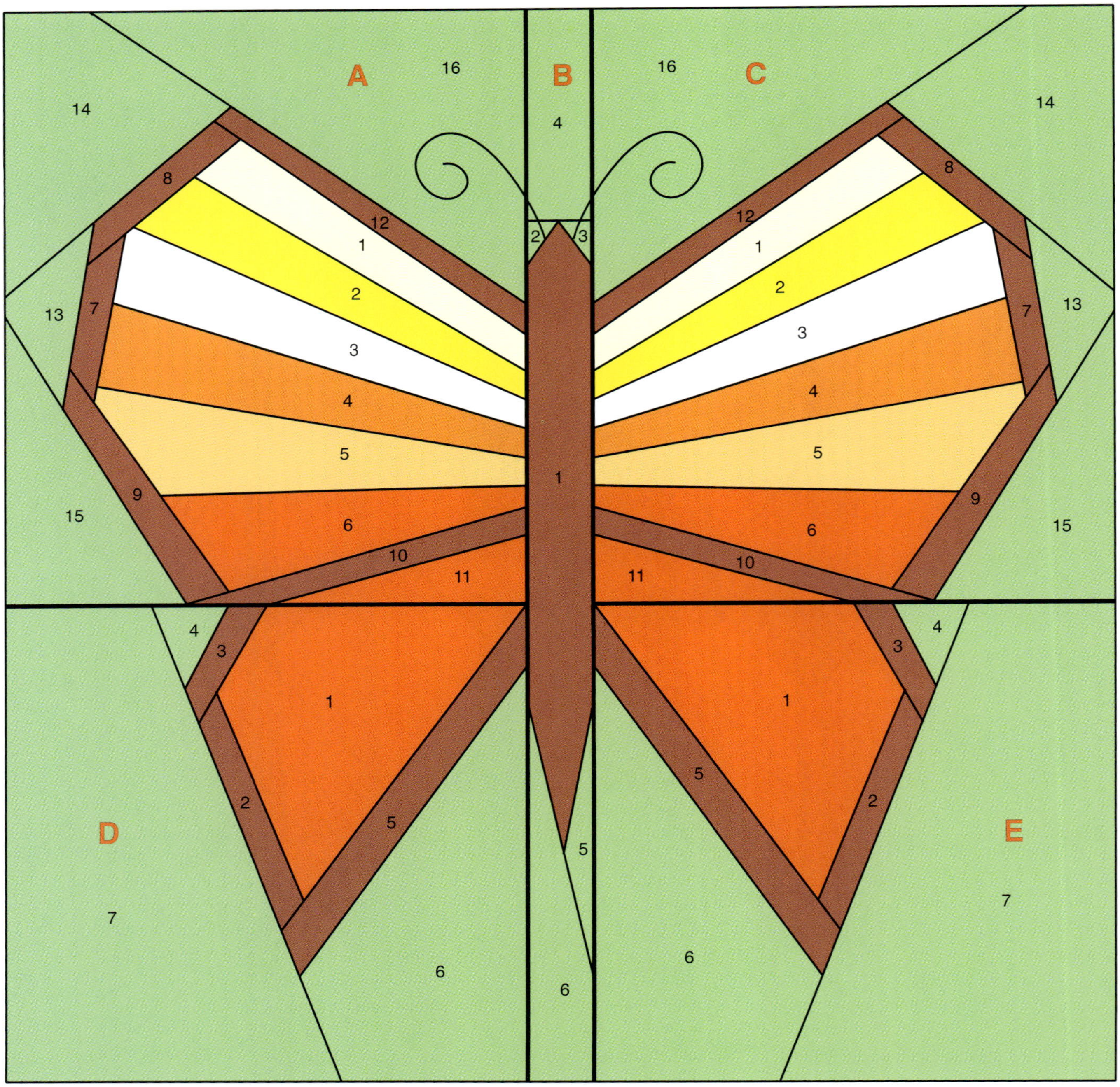

Butterfly

American School of Needlework • Berne, Indiana 46711 • DRGnetwork.com

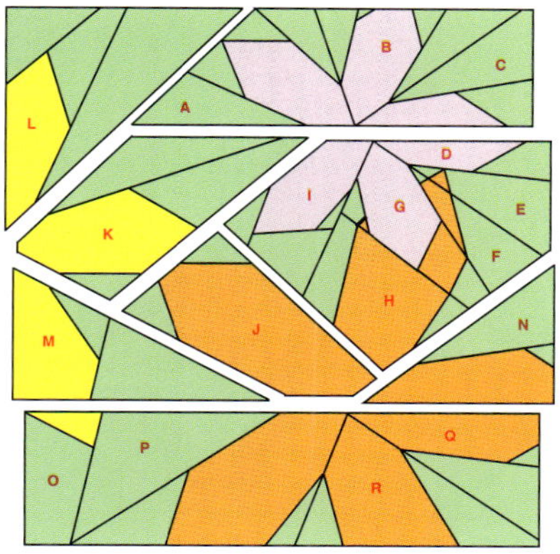

Flowers

Special note: *Attach seed beads to flower centers.*

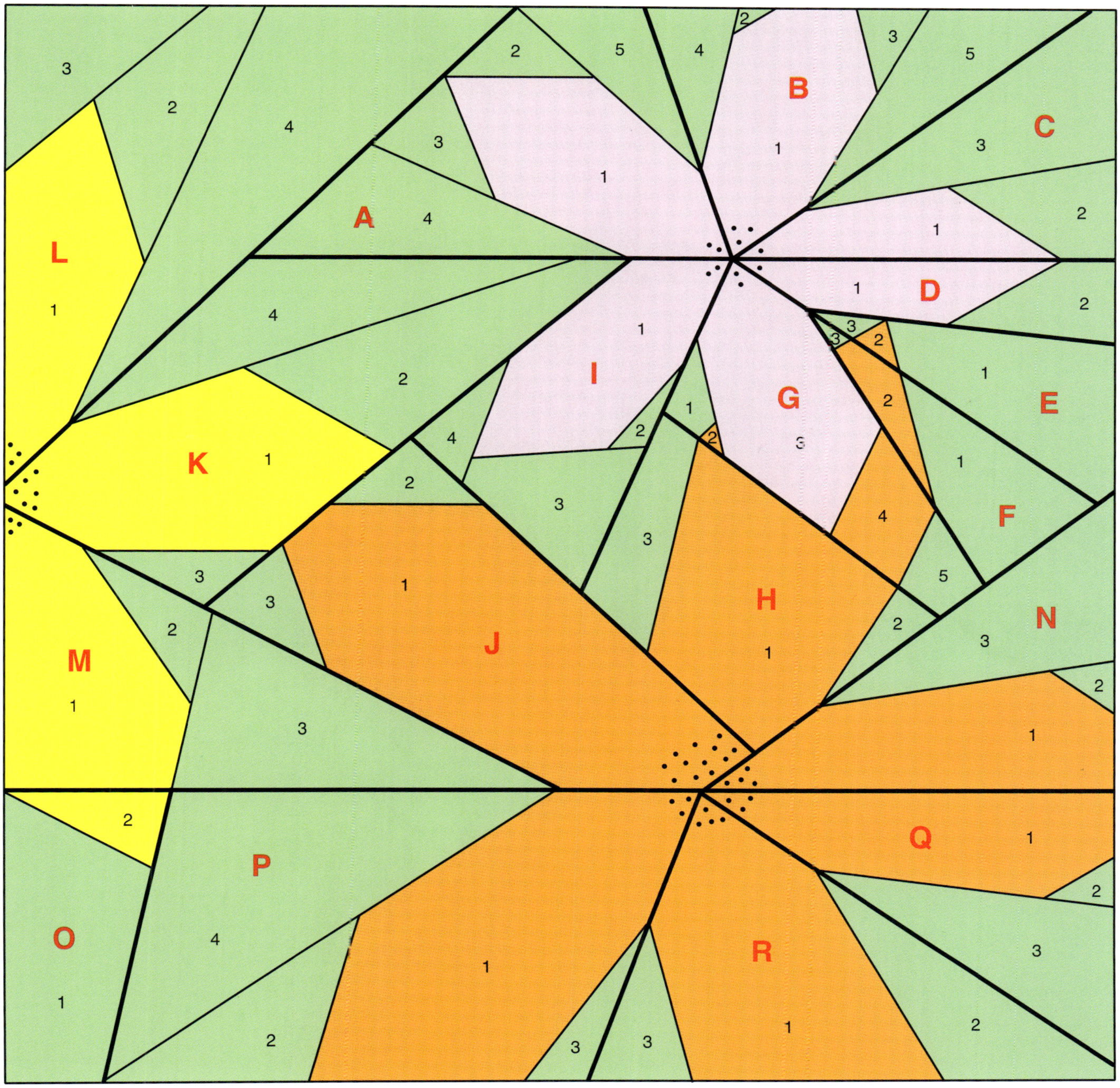

Flowers

Rocket

Special note: *Attach 2 pearl blue ¾-inch buttons for rocket windows.*

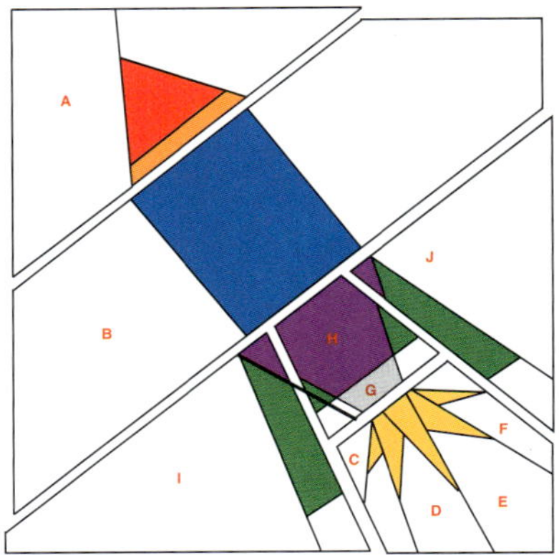

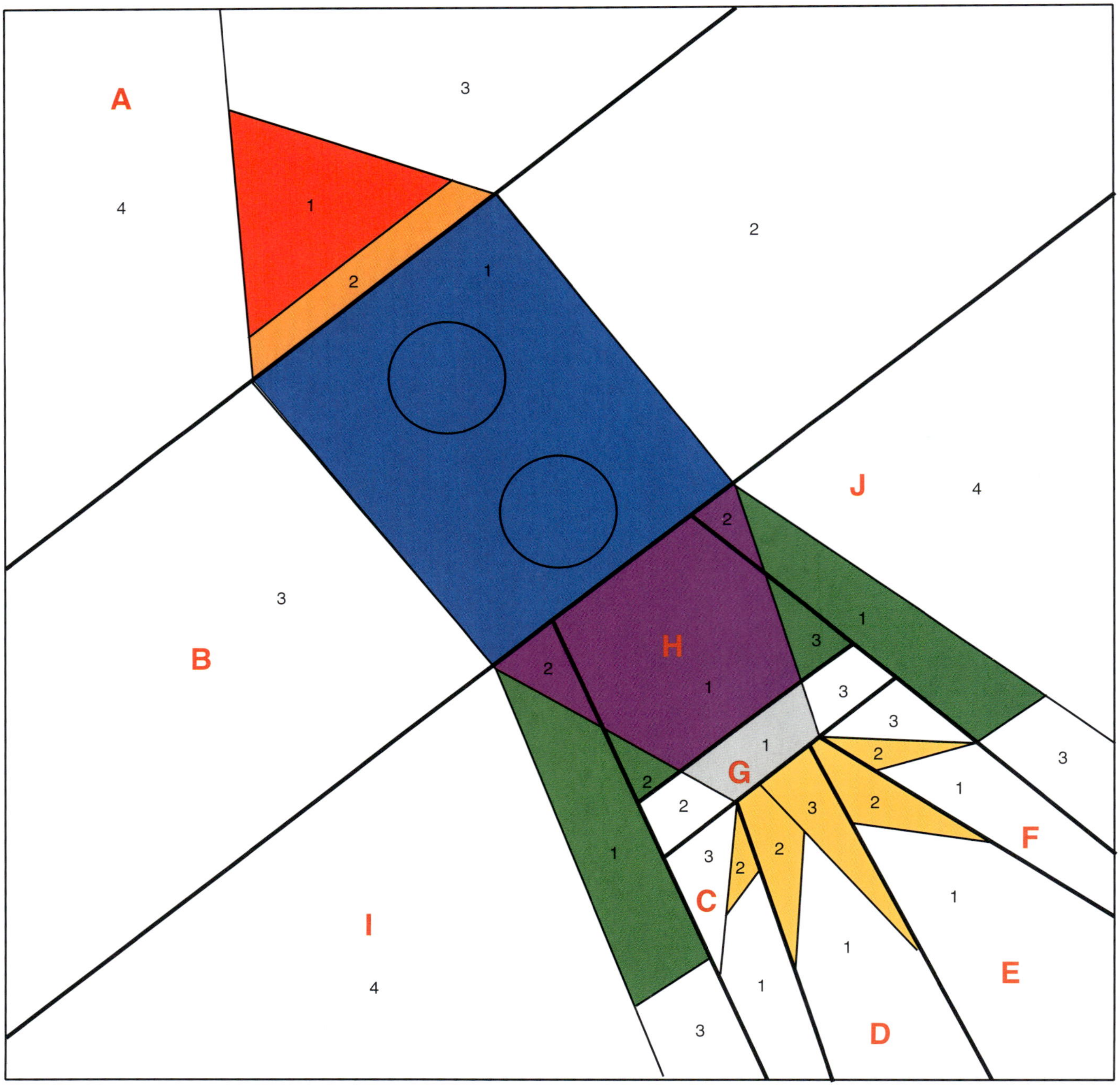

Rocket

American School of Needlework • Berne, Indiana 46711 • DRGnetwork.com

Sailboat

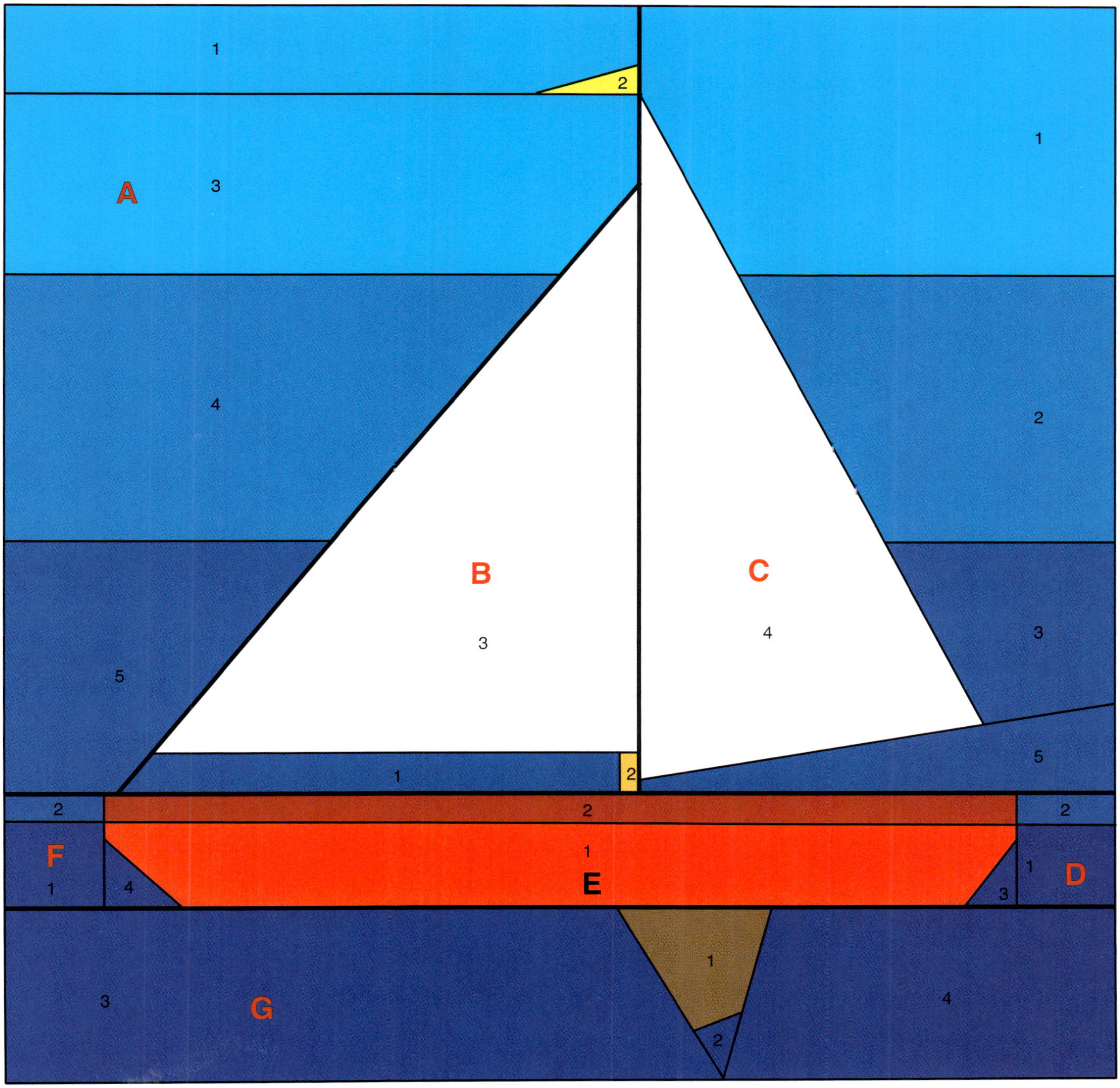

Sailboat

We wish to thank the following companies who generously supplied products for the projects:
Northcott/Monarch: cotton fabrics
Coats & Clark: cotton and metallic threads

TOLL-FREE ORDER LINE or to request a free catalog (800) 582-6643
Customer Service (800) 282-6643, **Fax** (800) 882-6643

Visit DRGnetwork.com.

ISBN: 978-1-59012-199-3 All rights reserved. Printed in USA 1 2 3 4 5 6 7 8 9